ESSENTIAL
QUEER
VOICES OF
U.S. POETRY

Also by Christopher Nelson

Blood Aria
Essential Voices: Poetry of Iran and Its Diaspora (editor)

Chapbooks
Fugitive
Love Song for the New World
Capital City at Midnight
Blue House

ESSENTIAL QUEER VOICES OF U.S. POETRY

Edited by Christopher Nelson
Introduced by Jack Halberstam

Green Linden Press

GREEN LINDEN PRESS
208 Broad Street South
Grinnell, Iowa 50112
www.greenlindenpress.com

Printed on recycled paper in the United States of America
First Edition

978-1-7371625-8-2

Library of Congress Cataloging-in-Publication Data

Names: Nelson, Christopher, 1975– editor.
Title: Essential queer voices of U.S. poetry / edited by Christopher Nelson.
Other titles: Essential queer voices of United States poetry
Description: First edition. | Grinnell, Iowa : Green Linden Press, 2024. |
Series: Essential voices ; 2 | "100 poets for the present and future" |
Identifiers: LCCN 2023022338 (print) | LCCN 2023022339 (ebook) |
ISBN 9781737162582 (paperback) | ISBN 9781737162599 (ebook)
Subjects: LCSH: American poetry—Sexual minority authors. | American
poetry—21st century. | LCGFT: Queer poetry.
Classification: LCC PS591.S4 E87 2024 (print) | LCC PS591.S4 (ebook) |
DDC 811.008/0920664—dc23/eng/20230728
LC record available at https://lccn.loc.gov/2023022338
LC ebook record available at https://lccn.loc.gov/2023022339

Cover and book design: Christopher Nelson

Green Linden Press is a nonprofit publisher dedicated to fostering
excellent poetry and supporting reforestation with a portion of proceeds.

Dedicated to
Maureen Seaton,
in memoriam

Contents

Editor's Note

The Essential Voices series intends to correct misrepresentation and misunderstanding in the broader culture. At its heart is the ancient idea that poetry can reveal our shared humanity. The first book in the series, *Essential Voices: Poetry of Iran and Its Diaspora*, received a Midwest Book Award and was named one of the best poetry books of 2021 by *Entropy Magazine*. Edited during the double nightmare of the COVID-19 pandemic and the Trump presidency, the anthology grew out of a desire to build a bridge to the Iranian people and cultures demonized or neglected by history, politics, and media. As an outsider to Iran and Persian literature—and it being my first anthology—the task was formidable. When the book was finished, I vowed to take a break before editing another, but that break lasted only three months.

As homo- and transphobia spread and heightened, and legislation against LGBTQ people became normal (the ACLU is tracking 496 such bills from this year alone), I felt compelled to assemble and share the work of one hundred poets who illuminate the queer experience in the United States, to present a fuller view, complex and true, as poetry does best. Gathered here are four generations of living writers, as varied in their subjects and styles as the nation they represent: rural, urban, young, old, academic, blue-collar, activist, domestic, cosmopolitan, local, brazen, subtle, out, and passing.

I grew up queer in a small, predominantly Mormon village. Life was pastoral and mostly lovely, and life was such that when Matthew Shephard's murder was in the news, I was sad but not surprised. I went to school with guys who displayed the same hatred. In the opening poem of this collection, "Queer," Frank Bidart writes,

> For each gay kid whose adolescence
>
> was America in the forties or fifties
> the primary, the crucial
>
> scenario
>
> forever is coming out—
> or not. Or not. Or not. Or not. Or not.

The same could be said for my 1990s adolescence, and while there has been significant progress made toward justice and acceptance for LGBTQ Americans, the same could be said for many today as well. A recent Boston University study showed that more people are coming out today, but queer suicide rates remain disturbingly high. It doesn't take a university study to know why. During the making of this book, I grieved for those murdered, injured, and traumatized in the Club Q massacre in Colorado Springs, and I couldn't help recall the horror of the 2016 Pulse nightclub massacre in Orlando, Florida, which a few of these poems address. As I write this, there is news of laws banning gender-affirming health care, news of a store owner shot and killed over a pride flag display, news of a young gay man stabbed to death while dancing outside a gas station. These ghastly things happen everyday; most don't make the news. I apologize for your entrée into this book being a bummer, but I believe that poets have the power—and the charge—to transform the vile into the sublime. The poems here do just that. I am honored to be their usher.

Physical violence isn't the only kind of violence, to be sure. The American Library Association reports that last year public and school libraries received a record-breaking 1,650 calls for elimination of books, with over a third of the targets featuring LGBTQ content. I'm calling this madness the Rainbow Scare—like the Red Scare we studied in school and many in this book lived through. In this discordant climate, this anthology is necessary—a rebuttal, a raised fist, but also a hello, a smile. It is my hope that these poems will be solace, beacon, beauty, lifeline, reprieve, solidarity, or at least entertainment for the millions of us against whom fascist forces have aligned. But this anthology isn't only for queer readers; as Diane Seuss writes in her endorsement, "This anthology is not representative of a sector of American poetry. It *is* American poetry." This points toward my ultimate hope for the book—an optimist's hope—that these poems facilitate seeing queerness as incidental to being human.

—Christopher Nelson

Queer Voices
by Jack Halberstam

Poetry does not tell stories, it gives shape to them. Poetry reveals the
limits to what can be told, illuminates the conventions of sense-making,
and, sometimes gently but often brutally, nudges new material from the
background to the foreground. Take CAConrad's gorgeous lyric from
Listen to the Golden Boomerang Return. The title, written in the imperative,
is an order as much as it is an invitation, but it is also a pedagogical note
on reading and poetry, order and disorder, and the hijacking of form. In
the poem, which sits on the page in the shape of an angled or fallen over
L, the poet begins at the end, the end of a sexual encounter in which two
lovers have been so deep inside each other that "we / heard / each / other
/ think." The impact of such sexual intensity between "queer pirates," we
are told, is to loosen in the poet "my wilderness." This space, an internal
not an external landscape, may well open onto utopia, but this ideal space
is not for frivolous activities such as "miscounting butterflies," it is a space
for making poems "that / can / rob / a bank." The boomerang of the poem
here flings thoughts and images and sensations out into space in the form
of a sexual encounter and then catches those same ideas on the return,
transformed by their journey and now visible as a commentary on poetry
itself. Poetry is a shape, a trajectory, a voice, many voices; it reaches for the
internal and then crushes the topography that had designated insides and
outsides. The poem returns as the potential for a crime, for transgression,
for theft.

What makes us think that poetry by queer and trans people has
much in common? Is this a poetry of transgressive sexuality? Are these
songs to bodily and psychic change? Do these poems form a lineage or
genealogy of some kind? I want to say no. Not because there are not all
kinds of shared themes in the poems, but because queerness itself is a
scattershot designation that sometimes means same-sex and at other times
indicates gender variations and often indicates secrecy or furtiveness or the
withholding of language altogether. The "essential poems" gathered here
then are not singing in the same key so much as all going in search of new
languages, "a common language" as Adrienne Rich put it many years ago.

Poetry shakes sense up and offers access to a new and uncommon language for queer life. In a poem taken from her extraordinary volume *feeld*, for example, Jos Charles reaches back into Middle English for a trans vocabulary and uses this strange but familiar English, an English bent by the passage of time, to disrupt the conventions of expression that produce simple narratives about transgender bodies. In so doing, Charles navigates the dangerous terrain of trauma and identity with restraint and formal complexity; she pulls away from cliché by making up a language and then slowly drawing us into it. And it is not just the phrasing or the words or the spelling or the syntax that Charles makes up or adapts from Medieval contexts. She also allows us to feel the assemblies that merge in Middle English, given that Medieval poetry may have been transcribed multiple times or translated or performed by many different people. Poems also arrive to the present with unknown provenance, orphaned and set adrift to make meaning with strangers. Charles pulls this understanding of poetry through her own and makes her poems thick with other people and also animals and landscapes. "I cant stop riting tran" reads one line, and "the feeld is an aeffect yes," reads another, reminding us that trans takes form against a field, a topography of gender, a field that might be full or fallow, a background that does not lie flatly behind the human who strides across it but that frames the human, gives her form and then absorbs her back into its folds. Charles explains that she sought a "colloquial language that is distinct from ours." A colloquial language distinct from ours—such a language estranges meaning and bodies while still presenting them in faintly recognizable forms. We see the trans in the feeld and the feeld in the "grl" and a reminder that it matters "how wee call a / thynge."

It matters, now more than ever, how and what and when we call a thing. As this book goes to press in 2023 in North America, how we call a thing has become the object of attention for conservatives looking to ban what they see as "gender indoctrination" in schools. This has led to book banning and the manipulation of curricula nationwide using the alibi of protecting children from unwelcome information about sexuality and gender. It mattered in the past too, how we called a thing, and terms like invert, pervert, transvestite, and others jostled for space in a medical lexicon, while words like pansy, dyke, butch, faggot, and punk found room to breathe in the social worlds built by queers and trans people. In medical and social science domains, old judgmental terminologies—effeminate—gave way to new liberal languages—gay and lesbian—and in queer and trans communities, generational shifts have spurred spats over terms that are favored in one era and decried in the next. But while social conservatives try to eliminate language, queer and trans poetry seeks expansion, new modes of expression, alternate codes for writing about the here, the now, the then, and the there.

These shifts in language, sensibility, and social meaning can be followed in John Keene's melancholic account of post-AIDS San Francisco. His poem "Mission and Outpost," which opens his acclaimed collection *Punks*, lays out in four-line stanzas a lost history as it subtends the present. Polk street here, and the Castro too, function as the "feeld," in Jos Charles's terms, for the poet's search for signs of the past. The poet considers his own queer education—"how to cruise and lay and lose the gold-tressed, / virile god of every queer boy's fantasies—but mine; bemoan // the arrival of one's sexual autumn, the dying light / of the Pines or dunes of Provincetown," lessons in how to love "young, tanned, muscular vapid beauties," but evidence too of the whiteness of the scene of encounter, then and now—a different kind of lesson in exclusion and indifference.

The queer worlds opened up by the poetry gathered here are not blameless or innocent, not revolutionary or reliably utopian. Just as CAConrad's utopian musings led to poems "that / can / rob / a / bank," so the former utopian spaces—Castro, the Pines, Provincetown—lead to the bank, to moneyed scenes where bankers and hustlers rub shoulders and more, exchange favors and more, and then who, in Keene's poem at least, often disappear or go mad… "or both." Keene turns away from the scene— "ratty white / twentysomething; a boohooing queen; a faun-haired boy / soon to turn his tail in porn to pay his rent"—and slips into the weather, "the steely, / spitty air." He is lost to history, lost in history, and cannot find the way back.

What is queer history? What is the transgender present? How does time shift and alter the meaning of these terms, and what from the past shuffles into the present moment where the poet finds a reader? There are so many of those moments gathered here. Marilyn Hacker's eulogy for Sára Karig, for example, "A Farewell to the Finland Woman," offers some conventional historical facts—"Two thousand orphans, real ones and children of / Jewish deported parents, so you and your / ill-sorted Red Cross wartime colleagues / made it your business to feed and save them" —but insists on details that escape the factual, details about lovers, about writing, about unnecessary mastectomies that nevertheless become part of the self—"When I knew you, you liked your flat chest"—details that link motherless women to childless butches in odd kinship arrangements. The orphans saved at the start of the poem come back by the end when one of them arrives to pay homage to the bravery of Karig and to present her with the novel the orphaned refuge has written. This "thank you," Hacker tells us, brings the "feeld" of kinship full circle: "motherless, childless, you made each other / possible. Without you, less is possible."

Without the poetry gathered here, truly, less is possible. As we witness new waves of conservative ideologies and new attempts to control the bodies of queer and trans children, we look for new ways to say who we are and who we are not. As younger people openly and loudly identify as queer, as trans, as nonbinary, and as they defy all attempts to silence them, they also articulate new languages of difference. When they say no to sexual and gender binarism, they also say no to the debt they are forced to carry, no to the corrupt political system, no to gay marriage as the only way to access shared benefits, no to corporate greed, no to the war on immigrants, no to white supremacy and police violence, no to real-estate capitalism. This no is both fierce and poetic.

Those loud "no's" and negation itself matter. In Robin Coste Lewis's poem "Lure," she rewrites history as a form of dissociation and negation: "I am not there," she proposes and then goes on to list all the things that did not happen in a childhood encounter with a sexually abusive relative. The things that did not happen to her are disavowed—"I am not three. I am not / breathing. I am not sitting in / your lap forgetting the body / has feet and legs and muscle / and sinew." And then she switches to the things that did not happen to the rapacious relative—"They did not / *not* kill you. Again and again. They did not / *not* slice your body into fine brilliant offerings." The double negative now confuses the unspooling intimate history from which the poet has dissociated herself. Did they kill him? Who? Is this a reference to a big "they," the "they" of white America? After the perpetrator has not not been killed, we return to the experience of dissociation that lodges itself in the girl's body as an alien presence that makes her incapable of saying what is and what is not: "This is not that feeling that / this is my body, / but I am somehow trapped inside / another girl, unable to say or feel a thing."

Lauren Berlant, in an essay titled "On Being in Life Without Wanting the World: No World Poetics, Or Elliptical Life," describes dissociation in these terms: "By dissociative life I mean a life lived in intimate relation to… a lifeworld that is also, and at the same time, apprehended ambivalently, from engaged distances, in an affective structure" where inhabitants of the no world "dwell in a detachment," but that detachment is not simply the "absence of feeling." Instead the feeling of detachment can be located in a "complex of lonelinesses."

Loneliness is not simply the feeling of being one instead of two or many. Loneliness is the feeling of being outside of the many. $X + Y - Y = X$.

Natalie Diaz might call this an "American Arithmetic." The poet cautions that "I'm not good at math" and then lays out the racial calculus of American life—the percentage of Native Americans likely to die at the hands of the police, the percentage of Native Americans in the population as a whole, the loss of life that was necessary for America to understand itself as white, and so on. She is not good at math, but the poet knows these calculations intimately, and she knows loneliness too—"I am begging: Let me be lonely but not invisible." Here, loneliness is all that lies between being and disappearing.

"But we r who we r," Tommy Pico reminds us. We r who we r—the feeld and the grl, the trans who cannot stop riting and the Black queer girl who is not not there. We are who we are, and who we are depends upon who you ask, and how the law judges you, and what crooks have been elected, and which stories cannot be told. Pico says, "Nothing can fall that wasn't built," and it is in the falling down that the nothing becomes worthy. A poem, Pico continues, "has to break you." The poems gathered here broke me. They break me, us, you, them. They break us apart, and nothing can fall that was not built, and nothing was built that cannot collapse, and in the ruins, in the rain, in the shadows of histories that refuse to be told, we read the poems that are capable of robbing banks.

ESSENTIAL
QUEER
VOICES OF
U.S. POETRY

Queer

*Lie to yourself about this and you will
forever lie about everything.*

Everybody already knows everything

so you can
lie to them. That's what they want.

But lie to yourself, what you will

lose is yourself. Then you
turn into them.

•

For each gay kid whose adolescence

was America in the forties or fifties
the primary, the crucial

scenario

forever is coming out—
or not. Or not. Or not. Or not. Or not.

•

Involuted velleities of self-erasure.

•

Quickly after my parents
died, I came out. Foundational narrative

designed to confer existence.

If I had managed to come out to my
mother, she would have blamed not

me, but herself.

The door through which you were shoved out
into the light

was self-loathing and terror.

•

Thank you, terror!

You learned early that adults' genteel
fantasies about human life

were not, for you, life. You think sex

is a knife
driven into you to teach you that.

Half-light

That crazy drunken night I
maneuvered you out into a field outside of

Coachella—I'd never seen a sky
so full of stars, as if the dirt of our lives

still were sprinkled with glistening
white shells from the ancient seabed

beneath us that receded long ago.
Parallel. We lay in parallel furrows.

—That suffocated, fearful
look on your face.

Jim, yesterday I heard your wife on the phone
tell me you died almost nine months ago.

Jim, now we cannot ever. Bitter
that we cannot ever have

the conversation that in
nature and alive we never had. Now not ever.

We have not spoken in years. I thought
perhaps at ninety or a hundred, two

broken-down old men, we wouldn't
give a damn, and find speech.

When I tell you that all the years we were
undergraduates I was madly in love with you

you say you
knew. I say I knew you

knew. You say
There was no place in nature we could meet.

You say this as if you need me to
admit something. *No place*

in nature, given our natures. Or is this
warning? I say what is happening now is

happening only because one of us is
dead. You laugh and say, Or both of us!

Our words
will be weirdly jolly.

That light I now envy
exists only on this page.

Frank Bidart

A Farewell to the Finland Woman

i.m. Karig Sára, 1917–1999

Sad is Eros, builder of cities
And weeping anarchic Aphrodite
   —W.H. Auden, "In Memory of Sigmund Freud"

Two thousand orphans, real ones and children of
Jewish deported parents, so you and your
   ill-sorted Red Cross wartime colleagues
   made it your business to feed and save them.

Black-out: You hacked up dray horses killed in the
air raids, and brought the meat to the orphanage:
   black market lamb a butcher comrade
   donated, you told suspicious children.

Interned in '53 as a Trotskyist
you underwent a double mastectomy
   for "lumpy breasts": chloroform was the
   one anesthetic used in the gulag.

Pain wasn't something you ever dwelled upon.
Most probably, your breasts weren't cancerous—
   Tubercular and convalescent
   you were excused from the mines and road work.

So you were put to work in the bindery.
You'd bound a Russian engineer's personal
   notebook in a silk scarf you'd hidden:
   proving your competence (proof you loved her)

and every evening, you warned the prisoners
who was in danger: punishment, overwork.
    You'd sworn, of course, you read no Russian
        —just a Hungarian female convict.

When I knew you, you liked your flat chest: you had
two inside pockets sewn in each suit jacket.
    You and the engineer exchanged long
        letters: your model for prose was Chekhov.

Your six-room Buda-side-of-the-Danube flat
reminded me of rooms in the Bronx which were
    East Europe reinvented, purplish
        overstuffed furniture, steamy laundry

hung in the bathroom on a contraption with
pulleys. You drank me under the table each
    night; I could hear you, every morning
        back at the typewriter at six-thirty.

What were you writing, decades of mornings when
you were a senior editor, polyglot
    translator, advocate for writers,
        war hero, fabulist, solitary—   ,

plays, novels, poems, autobiography?
Your published work: translations and book reviews—
    who'll tell what you would not have called your
        adventures, now that the typing's over?

You fell in love with Catherine the communist
Countess in Budapest, and you followed her
    back to the South of France. You called her
        Angel, she used your first name; gave orders.

Words were the way she let you make love to her.
She was a wicked octogenarian
    who'd flirt with anything that moved, but
    you were her Parsifal, chaste and loyal.

I met you there, one summer I worked at a
card table on a terrace that overlooked
    wild grapevines, fig trees, scrub oak, sheltered
    fluvial passage and small beasts' roving

—light years away from air raids, Siberia
and antebellum Marxist utopias
    you and your young friends once constructed
    late, in cafés, in your first, true language.

We spoke in English (French you disdained for an
unavowed reason: Vichy? The armistice?)
    She sometimes spoke to you in Russian,
    sometimes Hungarian, deep-voiced, urgent.

She took an overdose of barbiturates
the morning you were leaving for Switzerland
    together: she was ninety-two. You
    mourned her and put her affairs in order.

It was her daughter, eighty herself this year,
who told me that, this April, in Budapest
    you died, in the banal suburban
    site of your family-bound last exile.

One day, in '83 when I visited,
a dark-eyed, buxom, curly-haired novelist
    came with her newest book to give you,
    sat like a niece on the purple sofa.

She'd been a two-year-old in the orphanage:
her parents, Jewish deportees, left her there.
    You read her name forty years later
    on a much better list: writers' prizes.

But it was she remembered and searched for you,
insisted that you hear her encomiums.
    Partisan, scribe and second mother:
    motherless, childless, you made each other

possible. Without you, less is possible.
You'd disagree. Your monuments, elegies:
    heroes invent themselves from daily
    womanhood, though they lose breasts and borders.

Revolutionary Dreams

i used to dream militant
dreams of taking
over america to show
these white folks how it should be
done
i used to dream radical dreams
of blowing everyone away with my perceptive powers
of correct analysis
i even used to think i'd be the one
to stop the riot and negotiate the peace
then i awoke and dug
that if i dreamed natural
dreams of being a natural
woman doing what a woman
does when she's natural
i would have a revolution

Master Charge Blues

it's wednesday night baby
and i'm all alone
wednesday night baby
and i'm all alone
sitting with myself
waiting for the telephone

wanted you baby
but you said you had to go
wanted you yeah
but you said you had to go
called your best friend
but he can't come 'cross no more

did you ever go to bed
at the end of a busy day
look over and see the smooth
where your hump usta lay
feminine odor and no reason why
i said feminine odor and no reason why
asked the lord to help me
he shook his head "not i"

but i'm a modern woman baby
ain't gonna let this get me down
i'm a modern woman
ain't gonna let this get me down
gonna take my master charge
and get everything in town

That Day

if you've got the key
then i've got the door
let's do what we did
when we did it before

if you've got the time
i've got the way
let's do what we did
when we did it all day

you get the glass
i've got the wine
we'll do what we did
when we did it overtime

if you've got the dough
then i've got the heat
we can use my oven
til it's warm and sweet

i know i'm bold
coming on like this
but the good things in life
are too good to be missed

now time is money
and money is sweet
if you're busy baby
we can do it on our feet

we can do it on the floor
we can do it on the stair
we can do it on the couch
we can do it in the air

we can do it in the grass
and in case we get an itch
i can scratch it with my left hand
cause i'm really quite a witch

if we do it once a month
we can do it in time
if we do it once a week
we can do it in rhyme
if we do it every day
we can do it everyway
we can do it like we did it
when we did it
that day

Nikki Giovanni

But Since You Finally Asked

(A Poem Commemorating the 10th Anniversary of the Slave Memorial at Mount Vernon)

No one asked us ... what we thought of Jamestown ... in 1619 ... they didn't even say ... "Welcome" ... "You're Home" ... or even a pitiful ... "I'm sorry ... but we just can't make it ... without you" ... No ... No one said a word ... They just snatched our drums ... separated us by language and gender ... and put us on blocks ... where our beauty ... like our dignity ... was ignored

No one said a word ... in 1776 ... to us about Freedom ... The rebels wouldn't pretend ... the British lied ... We kept to a space ... where we owned our souls ... since we understood ... another century would pass ... before we owned our bodies ... But we raised our voices ... in a mighty cry ... to the Heavens above ... for the strength to endure

No one says ... "What I like about your people" ... then ticks off the wonder of the wonderful things ... we've given ... Our song to God, Our strength to the Earth ... Our unfailing belief in forgiveness ... I know what I like about us ... is that we let no one turn us around ... not then ... not now ... we plant our feet ... on higher ground ... I like who we were ...and who we are ... and since someone has asked ... let me say; I am proud to be a Black American ... I am proud that my people laboured honestly ... with forbearance and dignity ... I am proud that we believe ... as no other people do ... that all are equal in His sight ... We didn't write a constitution ... we live one ... We didn't say "We the People" ... we are one ... We didn't have to add ... as an after-thought ... "Under God" ... We turn our faces to the rising sun ... knowing ... a New Day ... is always ... beginning

Kay Ryan

Say Uncle

Every day
you say,
*Just one
more try.*
Then another
irrecoverable
day slips by.
You will
say *ankle,*
you will
say *knuckle;*
why won't
you why
won't you
say *uncle?*

Winter Fear

Is it just winter
or is this worse.
Is this the year
when outer damp
obscures a deeper curse
that spring can't fix,
when gears that
turn the earth
won't shift the view,
when clouds won't lift
though all the skies
go blue.

Ellen Bass

Mammogram Callback with Ultrasound

So this is what I'm here for, to see inside
the mute weight of my right breast, heavy handful
of treasure I longed for as a girl, crying
behind the curtain in the Guerlain sisters' corset shop.
Those tender spinsters could hardly bear
my tears, as they adjusted the straps
on a padded lace bra. I had to wait another year
before my breasts swelled like wind-filled sails
and many were the explorers carried away,
searching for perfumes and spices,
the nerve-laden nipples singing through the wires.
But never has there been a joy like this
as I lie in the pale green cool of radiology.
The lineage of death has swerved around me.
More happy love! More happy, happy love!
As the wand of the ultrasound glides over my flesh,
revealed is a river of light, a bright
undulant tangle of lobules and milk ducts,
harmless and radiant against the black fat.
I could be looking up at the night sky,
this wispy band of brilliance
a shining spur of the Milky Way galaxy,
and I, in my infinitesimal life, will,
at least for tonight, keep these lovely atoms
before I must return them to the stars.

Ode to Fat

Tonight, as you undress, I watch your wondrous
flesh that's swelled again, the way a river swells
when the ice relents. Sweet relief
just to regard the sheaves of your hips,
your boundless breasts and marshy belly.
I adore the acreage
of your thighs and praise the promising
planets of your ass.
O, you were lean that terrifying year
you were unraveling, as though you were returning
to the slender scrap of a girl I fell in love with.
But your skin was vacant, a ripped sack,
sugar spilling out and your bones insistent.
O praise the loyalty of the body
that labors to rebuild its palatial realm.
Bless butter. Bless brie.
Sanctify schmaltz. And cream and cashews.
Stoke the furnace
of the stomach and load the vessels. Darling,
drench yourself in opulent oil,
the lamp of your body glowing. May you always
flourish enormous and sumptuous,
be marbled with fat, a great vault that
I can enter, the cathedral where I pray.

Maureen Seaton

I'm watching *Argo* on the small screen and trying to write an erotic poem

about how I sat half-naked in the kitchen last night
while you cut my hair from waist to nape of neck,

trimming, shaping, hair falling quietly to the floor.
Watch out for nipples! I said, diverting your attention

for a split second, until you leaned in and kissed them.
Argo is almost completely devoid of the erotic, I notice—

screen shots of luscious architecture (minarets!) when
Affleck lands in Jordan, but that's about it. Now

I'm getting pissed off at *Argo*, every Iranian face
scripted to look mean, every American's scared or heroic.

Where's the sticky-finger baklava, the dove-blue mosque,
the grace and eros of a whole people censored

(cut!) along with any chance for poetry. (Reality.)
There was a moment when you held the mane of my hair

in your hand, inhaling, then swiveled me around to begin
the transformation. I forgot we're almost old enough

for those rocking chairs we once laughed about. On
the porch with our pups and the blankets across our laps.

Or, how about this? We're on that porch. You're playing
the devil out of a violin. I listen with my entire steamy soul.

The Sky Is an Elephant

—Jack Spicer (after Lorca), from "Ballad of the Little Girl
Who Invented the Universe"

Once I was the little girl who invented the universe.
I was sad as a chimney without a house.

I didn't mean this to be a poem, but it's building itself
And there is nothing I can do to stop it, truly, try

And stop me. I am sad as a house without a doll. See?
A doll without a mouth. A mouth without a smile. (Note

To poet: revise that last part, it's boring.) Here's a line
From Spicer or maybe Lorca—who cares? (They don't.)

But the sky is an elephant / and the jasmines are water without blood.
This is sad but it makes me happy, especially the elephant.

I think this poem actually ended somewhere around
The doll or the mouth, but I am too sad to fix it,

You know how that feels. So this makebelieve poem
Will go on as is, like the moon over the skeleton of a girl.

Jane Miller

Harmless Ode with Osip Mandelstam

When you are young you think everything
depends on the results
of one night

you bicycle home
late
in a white shirt

the air throws back
a song you're singing
no one is around

no someone's dog
is crying
following you

the cape curves
along a salty bay
gently

you follow the arc
of a good idea
with no horizon

in the off-season
the water appears
to have risen

a woman
made you feel
the immense

breathing far inside
a foghorn
every so often

when she came
you would pour her
liquid she would comb

you with long hair
you wheel so slowly
to stay the feeling

for the artist
there is the story
you are writing

and the story of writing it
when older
neither matters

the shooting stars
the silver bicycle
the shirt the streetlamps

forget as you forget
the desire that made you
dress and depart mysteriously

your soul
travels inward
time

is someone
with a hand down your throat
trying to dig out

what you sound like
alone
elusive as blue malva

sprinkled
over her bell
to arouse her

planted
on the grave
of the ancients

the dead feed
on the aphrodisiac
to return to form

its flower and leaf
salve each wound
of the nether world

the viscous heart
of the root
is a throat

emollient
to comfort the windpipe
on its journey from the lungs

listen
I have no notebooks
Mandelstam said

no manuscript and no archive
I alone in Russia work
from the voice

the artist has
but a few words
misted with steam

as pain clouds experience
to make plain
all is empty

all is luminous
the gears of illness
still

the wheels of drama
pause on the road planks
for you to fathom

the clear night
deep inside
as a Tang poet wrote

splatters of sudden rain
like pearls large and small
on a jade plate

Olga Broumas

Tryst

The human cunt, like the eye, dilates
with pleasure. And all by joy never named

now are priceless in the magnitude of the stars.
From are to are, have to have, beat sub-eternal.

By day, I found these on the beach, for you each
day and give. By night, remind me, I have

forgotten. Action replied by action, peace by peace.
Take you in all light and lull you on a sea

of flowers whose petals have mouths, mesmerized
centerfold, upsweep toward sleep.

She Loves

deep prolonged entry with the strong pink cock
the situps it evokes from her, arms fast
on the climbing invisible rope to the sky,
clasping and unclasping the cosmic lorus

Inside, the long breaths of lung and cunt
swell the vocal cords and a rasp a song,
loud sudden overdrive into disintegrate,
spinal melt, video hologram in the belly.

Her tits are luminous and sway to the rhythm
and I grab them and exaggerate their orbs.
Shoulders above like loaves of heaven,
nutmeg-flecked, exuding light like violet diodes

closing circuit where the wall, its fuse box,
so stolidly stood. No room for fantasy.
We watch ourselves transform the past
with such disinterested fascination,

the only attitude that does not stall
the song by an outburst of consciousness
and still lets consciousness, loved and incurable
voyeur, peek in. I tap. I slap. I knee, thump, bellyroll.

Her song is hoarse and is taking me,
incoherent familiar path to that self we are all
cortical cells of. Every o in her body
beelines for her throat, locked on

a rising ski-lift up the mountain, no
grass, no mountaintop, no snow.
White belly folding, muscular as milk.
Pas de deux, pas de chat, spotlight

on the key of G, clef du roman, tour de force letting,
like the sunlight lets a sleeve worn against wind, go.

Olga Broumas

Holes

Once when I passed East Fourth Street off First Avenue,
I think it was in early fall, and I had a small hole
in the shoulder of my white shirt, and another on
the back—I looked just beautiful. There was a
whole moment in the 70s when it was beautiful
to have holes in your shirts and sweaters.
By now it was 1981, but I carried that 70s style
around like a torch. There was a whole way of
feeling about yourself that was more European
than American, unless it was American around
1910 when it was beautiful to be a strong
starving immigrant who believed so much
in herself and she was part of a movement
as big as history and it explained the
hole in her shirt. It's the beginning
of summer tonight and every season has
cracks through which winter
or fall might leak out. The most perfect
flavor of it, oddly in June. Oh remember
when I was an immigrant. I took a black
beauty and got up from the pile of poems
around my knees and just had too much
energy for thought and walked over to
your house where there was continuous
beer. Finally we were just drinking
Rheingold, a hell of a beer. At the
door I mentioned I had a crush on both
of you, what you say to a couple. By
now the kids were in bed. I can't
even say clearly now that I wanted
the woman, though it seemed to be
the driving principle then, wanting
one of everything. I was part of

a generation of people who went to
the bars on 7th street and drank the
cheap whiskey and the ale on tap and dreamed
about when I would get you alone. Those
big breasts. I carried slim notebooks which only
permitted two or three-word lines. I need you.
"Nearing the Horse." There was blood in all my
titles, and milk. I had two bright blue pills
in my pocket. I loved you so much. It was
the last young thing I ever did, the end of
my renaissance, an immigration into my
dream world which even my grandparents
had not dared to live, being prisoners
of schizophrenia and alcohol, though
I was lovers with the two. The beauty
of the story is that it happened.
It was the last thing that happened
in New York. Everything else happened
while I was stopping it from happening.
Everything else had a life of
its own. I don't think I owe
them an apology, though at least
one of their kids hates my guts.
She can eat my guts for all
I care. I had a small hole in
the front of my black sleeveless
sweater. It was just something
that happened. It got larger
and larger. I liked to put
my finger in it. In the month
of December I couldn't get
out of bed. I kept waking
up at 6 p.m. and it was Christmas
or New Year's and I had
started drinking & eating. I remember
you handing me the most beautiful

Eileen Myles

red plate of pasta. It was like your cunt
on a plate. I met people in your house
even found people to go out and fuck,
regrettably, not knowing about
the forbidden fruit. I forget
what the only sin is. Somebody
told me recently. I have so
many holes in my memory. Between
me and the things I'm separated
from. I pick up a book and
another book and memory
and separation seem to
be all anyone writes
about. Or all they
seem to let me read.
But I remember those
beautiful holes on
my back like a
beautiful cloak
of feeling.

[I always put my pussy]

I always put my pussy
in the middle of trees
like a waterfall
like a doorway to God
like a flock of birds.
I always put my lover's cunt
on the crest
of a wave
like a flag
that I can
pledge my
allegiance
to. This is my
country. Here,
when we're alone
in public.
My lover's pussy
is a badge
is a night stick
is a helmet
is a deer's face
is a handful
of flowers
is a waterfall
is a river
of blood
is a bible
is a hurricane
is a soothsayer.
My lover's pussy
is a battle cry
is a prayer
is lunch

is wealthy
is happy
is on teevee
has a sense of humor
has a career
has a cup of coffee
goes to work
meditates
is always alone
knows my face
knows my tongue
knows my hands
is an alarmist
has lousy manners
knows her mind

I always put
my pussy in the middle
of trees
like a waterfall
a piece of jewelry
that I wear
on my chest
like a badge
in America
so my lover & I
can be safe.

Robin Becker

Dyke

The word came after me, then hid each time
I turned to look at it.
It breathed in the hedge. I could hear it bite
and snap the air.

I feared the woman with slicked-back hair
sitting on a bar stool,
her back to the dance floor, a beer in her hands.
Disco drove the word away

but it came back: *Bulldyke, Bulldagger.*
What did the word want
with me, and why this dread, this desire, this
dangerous butch

striding through Kenmore Square
uncamouflaged?
Dyke had a spike in it, a cleated surge.
In leathers, the word leapt

18th century grillwork
on the Boston Common and led the parade
around the city,
the slow, snaking, joyful, motorcade

of a new millennium. First
I had to hate her;
then I had to hurt her; the rest of my life,
I ate from her hand.

Late Apology

For betraying the potential depth
of character you saw in me, I apologize.
I apologize for *failing my pain.*
For having another woman in the wings.
For my febrile apologies, I apologize.
For the dinner parties I ruined
with my obsequious charm, my fabulist
stories more fiction than fact.
I apologize for making a scene
forty years ago at The Outdoor Store,
for not getting a grip, for my unexamined
angers. I apologize for choosing anger
instead of grief, for choosing rage
instead of laboring towards forgiveness.
I apologize for not pushing myself
harder, not doing the extra loop
at Fresh Pond and getting really winded.
Not sticking to the low-carb diet.
I apologize for calling the plumber
before trying to fix it myself, for expensive
hours on eBay looking at travel vests
with 16 pockets and Zuni beaded keychains,
for not being more like you, whom
I admire for your devotion to austerity
and for your excellent quads and calves
in the service of all things difficult.
I apologize for not giving you your due.
And for my mean-spirited imitations
of my former colleagues which often
embarrassed you and for my gift
for seeing the worst in people.
I'm sorry I didn't thank you for asking

more of me, thank you for staying
up late for our famous arguments, after which
each of us carried our burden of sadness—
you going up the mowing, me going down.

Initial Conditions.

Awakened by a herd of cows from sleeping pills that should have killed him.

Into inaccuracy.

The train, at a distance, pulling up the hill in advance of its noise.

This morning pelicans glide in formation across the glass tabletop at my side.

Corrected, slipping over the metal railing into the ocean.

Shame.

Wrapped in newspaper, behind a brick in the chimney, a canary inside a frayed blue purse inside a can.

A continual performance.

Love igniting that place in the caudate nucleus.

The day so searing, when walking from sunlight into the shade of a palo verde, I felt the cool glide up my shins as though I'd stepped into a pool of water.

The ghost had died, returning as a body.

Temporary.

The desperate will consider a boat made of ice.

The one in love, the fool, for whom the boundaries have disappeared.

The teacup spoke, the chair, the brass doorknob, the child ascribing consciousness to every object in the room.

You feel as though you play the role of nothing, that you fail to show up for your own life.

Having seen the stars once (the clouds closing over), the old man sailed (what else could he do?) as though he knew the coordinates.

Rebecca Seiferle

Florescence on 4th Avenue

Today it so happens I don't want to live, just as I'm going
into the native seed store, where the ancient seeds
of the world's various peoples are kept and sold
so they can perhaps root in tomorrow's ground, a young man
who was just on the other side of the street, yelling furiously
at his stoned friend on the other, quiets the raggedy
jingle jangle in his voice and crosses to ask me for a cigarette.
I light one for him, because he tries three times and, shaking,
keeps missing the flame, and it's enough time for me to see
clearly the blue ink someone scrawled all over his eyebrows
and temples, (though I cannot read what was written there,
on his skin, while he was passed out somewhere?)
and that his knuckles are scuffed open and bleeding.
It's obvious that he and his friend, following behind,
have been out here for a long time—at once each other's
family *and* enemy—that new social class—so many crazed
on the streets of America, it's as if an invisible war
in every school and house and neighborhood had cast out
its refugees. He's so roughed up, I'm a little afraid of him,
but he says: *How are you?* and I say, *OK, how about you,*
and he says, *I am tired of being here, I don't want to live, but here I am—*
stuck in this day, and suddenly he seems an omen, myself
drawing too near. The despair of every day buried
in all the so apparently functional people on this street,
not wanting to live but stuck in this day. So I'm glad
when he says *Thank you,* and I think to turn to the store
and its cultivations of every leaf and flower
that may soon go extinct. But he says insistently,
you're beautiful, and I think he's trying to hold on with flattery,
so I look at him, wryly, and he smiles, recognizing in me
his own strategies of evading the social lie. *No, I mean it...*
ma'am, and the *ma'am* deepens, and falls into feeling,

where all he is trying to say is *thank you*, a thank you
that arrives *bowing to one another in ashes, bowing
to the face of mercy in us, not yet, unutterably, torn.*

The Canary

So difficult to hear beyond the provisional racket
of the self, the small whisper of being,

yet sometimes I think, in the waking dream
after meditating, that I can feel the deepest pulse of all those I love,

slipping into a distant kitchen for a cup of water
or tripping down the morning stairs into the noise

of a different city, so far away, in whatever hour it is
wherever they are, that the pale flesh of an elbow

is so tangible and of such sweetness that it falls
as lightly as a hand placed on that acupressure point

that hurts above the heart. I don't know if it's
bodily memory falling as imperceptibly as

the gold pollen of the juniper tree, or the dream
of the cells of my body imagining

the world into flesh, some centerlessness
of being, but it's as piercing as the cry of the canary,

not the cultivated roller that sings with closed lips
in a cavernous cage while the waiters

in their white uniforms and hats marked "Mother's"
yell out orders and the names of customers—

the special of the day, a bowl full of trash, a cup
full of mud—until one hunches one's shoulders

and pitches into morning, but the original
nondescript green and yellow finch,

discovered in 1475 on the "Isle of Dogs," which sang
only when it was alone, a song so piercing

because it had to travel across
all the distances of the world.

David Trinidad

Counting My Scars

1) The faint white circle
   on my forehead where
   a wart was removed.

2) The indentation in my left cheek
   (most noticeable when I smile)
   where, as a toddler, I fell and hit
   the corner of our coffee table.

3) The scar on my chin
   I got in high school—
   eight stitches, as I recall.
   After a friend and I smoked
   a joint in his garage,
   I stood up too fast, blacked
   out, and fell chin first
   on the cement floor.
   My friend handed me
   a greasy rag to stop
   the blood pouring down
   my neck. My mother
   found a doctor who
   would see us after hours.
   As he sewed the wound,
   he let me know that he
   knew that I was stoned.

4) The excision on the left side of my neck
   where they took out a pre-cancerous mole.
   Like a child, I rewarded myself afterwards,
   with a plastic glow-in-the-dark candlestick from
   the Museum of Contemporary Art's gift shop.

5) The discolored mark
   in the middle of my left
   ring finger, where my brother
   stabbed me with a pencil.
   We were arguing over whose
   turn it was to sleep in the
   top bunk. I've carried this lead
   with me my entire life.

6) The white cross-shaped scar
   on my left wrist. From the car
   accident in 1979. Where the IV
   was inserted and taped in place.

7) The Frankenstein-esque scar
   down the middle of my stomach,
   also from the accident. From
   the removal of my spleen.

8) Another Frankenstein-esque scar,
   also from the accident, that starts
   in front and wraps around my left side,
   onto my back. From a collapsed lung.

9) The line across my pelvis
   (hidden by pubic hair) from
   the repair of a double hernia.
   In the recovery room, they
   kept making me drink water,
   as they wouldn't release me
   until I peed. It hurt to walk,
   worse to urinate. Climbing
   the two flights of stairs to
   my loft was one of the most
   difficult things I've ever had

to do. I spent a week (at least)
on the couch in the living room,
sleeping and watching movies
on TV. Trust me, *Who's Afraid
of Virginia Woolf?* on Vicodin
is a special kind of insane.

10) The dark crescent—again from
the accident—that runs the length
of my left tibia. The bone, I was
told, "snapped like a branch."
It was mended with a metal plate.
Which they removed a year later.
Before the operation, as I lay on
a gurney, tears streamed down the
side of my face. When he came
to put me under, the doctor wiped
them away and said, "You're very
brave." Then: "You're going to feel
a prick." Which, being gay, made me
laugh. Then everything went black.

The Boy

Looking back,
I think that he must have been an angel.
We never spoke,
but one entire summer, every day,
he sat on the curb across the street.
I watched him: thin, his skin white,
his blond hair cut short.
Sometimes, right after swimming,
his bathing suit wet and tight,
he would sit and dry off in the sun.
I couldn't stop staring.

Then late one night,
toward the end of the summer,
he appeared in my room.
Perhaps that's why
I've always considered him
an angel: silent, innocent, pale
even in the dark.
He undressed
and pulled back the sheet,
slid next to me.
His fingers felt for my lips.

But perhaps I am not remembering
correctly.
Perhaps he never came
into my room that night.
Perhaps he never existed
and I invented him.
Or perhaps it was me, not blond
but dark, who sat all summer

on that sunny corner: seventeen
and struggling to outlast
my own restlessness.

David Trinidad

Mark Doty

Charlie Howard's Descent

Between the bridge and the river
he falls through
a huge portion of night;
it is not as if falling

is something new. Over and over
he slipped into the gulf
between what he knew and how
he was known. What others wanted

opened like an abyss: the laughing
stock-clerks at the grocery, women
at the luncheonette amused by his gestures.
What could he do, live

with one hand tied
behind his back? So he began to fall
into the star-faced section
of night between the trestle

and the water because he could not meet
a little town's demands,
and his earrings shone and his wrists
were as limp as they were.

I imagine he took the insults in
and made of them a place to live;
we learn to use the names
because they are there,

familiar furniture: *faggot*
was the bed he slept in, hard
and white, but simple somehow,
queer something sharp

but finally useful, a tool,
all the jokes a chair,
stiff-backed to keep the spine straight,
a table, a lamp. And because

he's fallen for twenty-three years,
despite whatever awkwardness
his flailing arms and legs assume
he is beautiful

and like any good diver
has only an edge of fear
he transforms into grace.
Or else he is not afraid,

and in this way climbs back
up the ladder of his fall,
out of the river into the arms
of the three teenage boys

who hurled him from the edge—
really boys now, afraid,
their fathers' cars shivering behind them,
headlights on—and tells them

it's all right, that he knows
they didn't believe him
when he said he couldn't swim,
and blesses his killers

in the way that only the dead
can afford to forgive.

Homo Will Not Inherit

Downtown anywhere and between the roil
of bathhouse steam—up there the linens of joy
and shame must be laundered again and again,

all night—downtown anywhere
and between the column of feathering steam
unknotting itself thirty feet above the avenue's

shimmered azaleas of gasoline,
between the steam and the ruin
of the Cinema Paree (marquee advertising

its own milky vacancy, broken showcases sealed,
ticketbooth a hostage wrapped in tape
and black plastic, captive in this zone

of blackfronted bars and bookstores
where there's nothing to read
but longing's repetitive texts,

where desire's unpoliced, or nearly so)
someone's posted a xeroxed headshot
of Jesus: permed, blonde, blurred at the edges

as though photographed through a greasy lens,
and inked beside him, in marker strokes:
HOMO WILL NOT INHERIT. *Repent & be saved.*

I'll tell you what I'll inherit: the margins
which have always been mine, downtown after hours
when there's nothing left to buy,

the dreaming shops turned in on themselves,
seamless, intent on the perfection of display,
the bodegas and offices lined up, impenetrable:

edges no one wants, no one's watching. Though
the borders of this shadow-zone (mirror and dream
of the shattered streets around it) are chartered

by the police, and they are required,
some nights, to redefine them. But not now, at twilight,
permission's descending hour, early winter darkness

pillared by smoldering plumes. The public city's
ledgered and locked, but the secret city's boundless;
from which do these tumbling towers arise?

I'll tell you what I'll inherit: steam,
and the blinding symmetry of some towering man,
fifteen minutes of forgetfulness incarnate.

I've seen flame flicker around the edges of the body,
pentecostal, evidence of inhabitation.
And I have been possessed of the god myself,

I have been the temporary apparition
salving another, I have been his visitation, I say it
without arrogance, I have been an angel

for minutes at a time, and I have for hours
believed—without judgement, without condemnation—
that in each body, however obscured or recast,

is the divine body—common, habitable—
the way in a field of sunflowers
you can see every bloom's

the multiple expression
of a single shining idea,
which is the face hammered into joy.

I'll tell you what I'll inherit:
stupidity, erasure, exile
inside the chalked lines of the police,

who must resemble what they punish,
the exile you require of me,
you who's posted this invitation

to a heaven nobody wants.
You who must be patrolled,
who adore constraint, I'll tell you

what I'll inherit, not your pallid temple
but a real palace, the anticipated
and actual memory, the moment flooded

by skin and the knowledge of it,
the gesture and its description
—do I need to say it?—

the flesh *and* the word. And I'll tell you,
you who can't wait to abandon your body,
what you want me to, maybe something

like you've imagined, a dirty story:
Years ago, in the baths,
a man walked into the steam,

the gorgeous deep indigo of him gleaming,
solid tight flanks, the intricately ridged abdomen—
and after he invited me to his room,

nudging his key toward me,
as if perhaps I spoke another tongue
and required the plainest of gestures,

after we'd been, you understand,
worshipping a while in his church,
he said to me, *I'm going to punish your mouth.*

I can't tell you what that did to me.
My shame was redeemed then;
I won't need to burn in the afterlife.

It wasn't that he hurt me,
more than that: the spirit's transactions
are enacted now, here—no one needs

your eternity. This failing city's
radiant as any we'll ever know,
paved with oily rainbow, charred gates

jeweled with tags, swoops of letters
over letters, indecipherable as anything
written by desire. I'm not ashamed

to love Babylon's scrawl. How could I be?
It's written on my face as much as on
these walls. This city's inescapable,

gorgeous, and on fire. I have my kingdom.

[I met a man]

I met a man who was a woman who was a man who was a woman
who was a man who met a woman who met her genes who tic'd the
toe who was a man who x'd the x and xx'd the y I met a friend who
preferred to pi than to 3 or 3.2 the infinite slide through the river of
identitude a boat he did not want to sink who met a god who was a
tiny space who was a shot who was a god who was a son who was a
girl who was a tree I met a god who was a sign who was a mold who
fermented a new species on the pier beneath the ropes of coral

I met a man who was a fume who was a man who was a ramp who
was a peril who was a woman who carried the x and x'd the y the yy
who xx'd the simple torch

I rest (the man who) a woman who tells the cold who preferred a
wind who was a silo a chime who met a corner a fuel an aurora a hero
a final sweep

[I give myself / the same seven / minutes]

I give myself
the same seven
minutes and close
my eyes inside
the old refrigerator
hum that takes
the contents
of my heart
and pours
them into
the morning
I think to make
something as
precious as you
so my fingers
begin to perform
but I hate to perform
so my hands rebel
and take me back
to bed to be
with you
new creature
of this world
so much like
a tree or closer
to a sapling
or a seed
your entire
life manifest
in the silence
of the bedroom
and the whoosh
of your heart

Samuel Ace

in your rest I
touch your side
and you already
know to stretch
into my hand
eyes wide open
as serious as
the eucalyptus
at the corner
of the house
two doors down
you stare at
and through me
to where no one
and nothing performs
dear daughter
of creation
how do
you know
to do this
how does
a seed know
the largest branch
the respiration
of the planet?

Barbara Cully

The ceaseless turning

...has ended in flowers. —*Pablo Neruda*

My cup my knight my crow my love
    this prosey tale is dreaming.

This cup my knight my crow my love
    the return of the animal to the mineral.

This cup my knight my crow my love
    zero over my zero,
    fossil etched,
    were I not loved.

This cup my knight my crow my love
    spoken as
    this wheel as ache
    and prayed for once.

My cup my knight my crow my love
    you have it
    near at hands,
        earth-urn,
    as what you
    but love.

My cup my knight my crow my love
    whilst
    you let it tilt,
        global
        lessed
    you did hear it mown
    leafy let fall
    as one put turning.

My cup my knight my crow my love
    leafy let fall
    dissed not
    joke knot
    of ceaseless
    what…
            it audible,
            it turning.

My cup my knight my crow my love
    words in sutures
    where once was put,
            as once in-toned,
    spike of want…
    you spoke it
            singing.

My cup my knight my crow my love
    leafy let curve
    this ashen orchard mound
    ghost garland grove…
            and morn
    is misting.

My cup my knight my crow my love
    desist
    less
    at heart end
    and bloom
            he said
    it turning.

Natasha Sajé

Tinguage

hapax legomenon

What you do to me. With me. What I've
Learned to do with you. A language
Of bliss, a sublingual, interlingual,
Bilingual tale that lasts from labial
Lark through the long light of dawn.
A trickle of terroir layered in taste, liquid
As thirst. More than touch, less than labor,
This lesson in tilt and lather. The tang of a lyre
Of skin, a lick of liberal tact in tandem.
Our own *langue d'oc*, turtled in time
And tinkered by thrill. It's not lex, not law—
But logos, the tabor and talisman of love.

Essay on Touch

Not unlike the trapped wolf that chews
its leg free, a doctor at the South Pole
operates on her own breast

instructed via satellite.
Any EMT can tell you that
placing a hand on the face

of shock victims calms their wild hearts.
Once when a child kept kicking
my airplane seat I put an illegal

hand on his ankle and made a lethal
threat. I'm not usually so powerful.
I can't keep coyotes from killing

my cats nor deer from my tulips. What
kind of deterrent is human hair?
A nearly blind student told me

her mother shook her so hard, her
retinas detatched—and said this
as if she were mentioning her brand

of shampoo. Nurses know it's friction—
not just soap—that kills microbes, and it takes
a full minute to do it right. That's

singing "happy birthday" twice,
or one-eighth of "MacArthur Park."
When my father was dying I could

only stroke his arms and wait, and wish
I'd done more of that before.
Drug deals and shootings take place

in sunny daylight while I'm baking
Cassata Siciliana with green tea almond icing
that I've rolled out to the thickness

of a dime. I'd gladly offer it
to hungry animals—
or you, reader, if only you'll stay

and place your open mouth on mine.

Dear Fisher Cat (*Martes Pennanti*),

Never seen you in the flesh. I've seen
a cousin, *martes martes*, stuffed, in a shop window
in Bavaria, where they chew wiring in cars,
and *martes zibellina* turned
into a coat, thicker than mink, the price of a house.
I tried it on, with awe.
I watched *martes fiona* on YouTube,
the woman holding the camera cooing
while the small, shy animal
nosed around her terrace in the English countryside.
Your name in Croatian, Kuna, is currency.
Seven million years old, much older than *homo*,
and certainly *sapiens*. Trapped to the brink
of extinction, you came back.
You are to the others as the javelina is to the wild boar,
a new world clade. Neither fisher nor cat.
Some people love bears or whales
or whooping cranes; I love you:
your sweet round ears and button nose,
your fur heavy as the robe of a queen,
your claws unsheathed in paws
the size of a child's hand. You could be a toy, a cartoon,
a pet, if it weren't for your carnivorous drive,
your solitary soul. Your jaws can kill a porcupine,
attacking snout first from below, eating it inside
out. You cross the narrowest
gap in the forest opening. You sleep in the crook
of a beech in old growth canopy. I'll see you someday,
close range. I'll be the rabbit
curled in a corner of the parsley garden
and you—you'll be there, unnoticed
until too late, to swallow all the sounds my gullet makes.

Henri Cole

Doves

Gray and white, as if with age, or some preserving
of the past, as in Beowulf, our hoary ancestor,
hoary as in a bat or a willow, or the venerable
hoary dove that flew straight into my picture
window today and then lay dead on the front porch.
We buried it—in some distorted version of its normal self—
folded in a white cloth napkin in the backyard.
Still soft enough to be cut into like a cabbage, I thought,
I'm glad I'm not dead. Listen to them now,
higher up in the trees, biting and scratching,
with their unmistakable twitch of life. *Don't fear
nothing,* their twittering voices cry. The true spirit
of living isn't eating greedily, or reflection, or
even love, but dissidence, like an axe of stone.

American Kestrel

I see you sitting erect on my fire escape,
plucking at your dinner of flayed mouse,
like the red strings of a harp, choking a bit
on the venous blue flesh and hemorrhaging tail.
With your perfect black-and-white thief's mask,
you look like a stuffed bird in a glass case,
somewhere between the animal and human life.
The love word is far away. Can you see me?
I am a man. No one has what I have:
my long clean hands, my bored lips. This is my home:
Woof-woof, the dog utters, afraid of emptiness,
as I am, so my soul attaches itself to things,
trying to create something neither confessional
nor abstract, like the moon breaking through the pines.

Cyrus Cassells

Mirtiotissa!

When I spotted eye-catching Stavros,
A man on a joyous carousel:
He was comically saddled
On a cartoon racehorse
With his loudly clapping five-year-old son,
Bobbing up and down
To the loopy music of a calliope
(How do you say *giddyup* in Greek?);
I was entranced, of course,
By his clear-to-all tenderness
And unabashed laughter,
And his puissant, lucid-blue gaze,
Like a salvo—
Tell me, are you a tourist? Yes?
Then you must come to my restaurant
On a hill beside the New Fortress;
Don't forget. Here's my card—

If the evening tables weren't too busy
In his terrific seafood tavern,
Caring Stavros would pause to chat
With "Captain America"
(As he quickly christened me)
Sometimes until closing—
There was a carefree aura
About our late-night talks
And occasional strolls
Through Corfu Town's vital labyrinth:
Balmy, centering, and arousing
In almost the same breath—
That's how I discovered appealing Stavros hailed
From Thessaloniki, not the island—
When he gallantly elected to help me

Improve my less-than-stellar swimming:
Captain America,
It's my specialty, he proclaimed—
As a desert-raised military brat,
I'd learned much too late
To fully tackle the agile butterfly
And essential breaststroke—
So solicitous Stavros,
Once Olympics-headed in his teens,
Offered to instruct me—
A felicitous gesture because
"Stavros is the best swimmer on Corfu,"
Insists his bearded painter friend,
Whom everybody calls Big Iraklis—

Stavros was infinitely courteous, easygoing,
Calmly working with me in a hotel pool,
Until he suggested swimming lessons
At a few western beaches:
Yialiskari, Halikounas, Vatos,
And after a month of exploring
Those genial out-of-town settings,
He finally said: *It's time to hit*
The nude beach, Mirtiotissa;
I hope that's not a problem—

At Mirtiotissa, the shoreline stones
Were just lackluster stones,
Till, in a sorcerer's flash, the tide claimed
Their black and pell-mell pewter—
The high, rugged cliffs,
The multicolored water shimmered,
While the bellicose morning fumed,
Almost sauna-hot,
So the only recourse was to jettison
Our cumbersome shorts

And flower-patterned trunks and welcome
Mirtiotissa's almost lukewarm waves,
Rife with darting, migratory fish—

We strolled past what Stavros tagged
"The textile guests,"
The old sarong-sporting
Hippie survivors from the 80s
When the tantalizing beach
Was much wider—and,
According to local gossip, wilder.
It felt truly liberating
To practice our usual strokes,
Unhampered by any trunks.
While his sidekick Big Iraklis
Dozed and tanned on the shore,
Delightful Stavros, minus his clothing,
Was consistently quiet,
Tranquil, and undaunted, confiding:
I feel happy as a clam,
As you English speakers say—

We rested a little after my lesson,
Then Stavros said: *Come, let me show you*
A cave I've found; it's really quite something.
We can leave Mr. Big-Ass Iraklis behind
To sleep and snore.

There were just enough holes
In the outlying cave's rough ceiling
To approximate natural skylights,
So the hovering sun cast a spotlight
To emphasize Stavros's face and cheekbones
As he whispered,
Since you met me with my son,
I'm sure you imagined

I had no desire for you
Or other men, but I do;
I brought you here because…

There was no resisting courteous Stavros then,
His blue-green, un-ignorable gaze,
His strong, stubble-dotted jaw,
His half-moon scar complicating
His film-star-ideal cleft chin,
His drying torso, still glistening from the sea,
His hardy, suddenly encircling arms,
His white-as-a-hospital-ward teeth,
His insistent lips at my ear's curve,
His cologne-flecked nape and Adam's apple,
His questing, failsafe tongue,
His commanding kisses,
His formidable shoulders and biceps (his biceps!),
His diamond-shaped birthmark almost covering
His left armpit (the sweat and seaside musk my nostrils find there)
His broad chest, meant for worshipping,
His aureoles like bronze zeroes, excavated coins,
His sea-wet nipples like small swart summits,
His salt-tasting index finger between my mock-biting teeth,
His cable-taut thighs, marvelous pillars,
His able cock, arriving like an astute animal—

I heard a sibilant gull's cry and susurrus,
And sensed someone else
Looming in the cave:
Beautiful, Big Iraklis whispered,
Oh, baby, be good to Stavros.
Captain America, do you mind if I watch
And touch you, too?
Iraklis, the gate-tall tagalong, whom I figured
Was mostly indifferent to me!
Admission: his outsized penis

Felt almost amiable at first,
At rest on my sienna-skinned shoulder,
Then thick and thicker
In my grasping hand—

After laving away
Pale pennants from the little battlefield
Of my glistening belly, souvenirs
Of our unhampered horseplay,
At dusk, suddenly dwarfed
By the evening sky,
We danced at the sea-lip
With some newfound friends
To Stavros's many catchy tapes
(*What is this,* I laughed,
Greek Soul Train?), and once,
Between irresistible songs,
And a wild, free-form summer *sirtaki*
(*I'm the king of the castle;*
You're the dirty rascal!),
He whispered:
If you're wondering, I didn't plan on
The three of us in the cave,
But Big Iraklis is always restless,
Curious. And of course,
He was a little jealous!
Now to my real question: it's only
The middle of summer, so you'll still need
More swimming lessons, right?
And our busy painter's suddenly ready
To paint your portrait—
I wonder why!
Knowing him, he'll probably splash
More paint on your American flesh
Than on his waiting canvas!—
So, dear Captain, you must come see us!

More than half-intoxicated,
Weed-struck, an ecstatic Stavros
Rushes in my direction,
Waving the white spine
Of some poor, luckless fish
Like an irreverent movie prop,
Hollering, chanting, almost singing:
Mirtiotissa, Mirtiotissa!
I'm crazy for Mirtiotissa!
With a ribald jester's, a truant's
Face-splitting grin,
Elm-strong Iraklis blurts:
Captain America, for sure,
I'm pretty large down there—
You know, that's how I got
My nickname—so I have to say
I'm impressed!
Have no doubt, as Stavros told you,
I'm planning to do your portrait,
So let's have another round
Of ouzo, or maybe your prefer retsina.
Let's drink a toast to Stavros's "special cave."
Let's drink a toast to Mirtiotissa!

Janet McAdams

The Way the World Comes Back

When did you notice it was no longer winter?
Skin sloughing away after the dry cold?
Or the moment you shed
the heavy coat you wear against the world?

This paring down is no small matter.
The urge to crack and cast away
the shell the body forged from years of grief.
The way the knife can't help but slip
and so much of the work must be done at twilight.

But what if the world came back?
Even in miniature or scarred.
Lush green or bruised yellow,
wind strong enough to lift feather or leaf,
unravel the long scarf from your throat,

to sweep the dust from stone,
uncover bone or story.
What if your stone heart turned to salt?
What if it turned to water
and roared through your body like an ocean?

Ghost Ranch

Light picks this landscape down to bone.
It's Boxing Day. The orange jumpsuits
six miles back pick trash while they do time.
The guards in their blue suits are white.
Someone has cut the Indian prisoners' hair.

The mesa's one short hard haul straight up.
Gray feather in the crack I work my fingers
into and tug and work them out again.
Then flat on top and land for miles and miles—
so much land. You find a pile of bones

and hold the pelvis up to frame a ragged disc
of sky. Not the real sky, I thought that day,
but blue enough to tell this story. You say
the feather's from a dove and spot an eagle
circling high across the canyon, but I am not

so sure. We touch and circle and touch and circle
until we only circle: cloth against cloth, skin
not quite meeting, the way fences touch at the corners
of nations. Last night you slept so quietly,
I put a hand to your back to make sure

you were breathing, the other over your shoulder
and flat against the skin between nipple
and solar plexus: because breath may not be
a sure enough measure. We hover
over the animal that carved itself

this place to rest, past molecule, atom,
the stinging energy that drums the universe
into being. Don't say you never felt it.
Even the stone was pulsing. Take my hand
if you can bear it, but let the other story go.

The Aureole

(for E)

I stop my hand midair.

If I touch her there everything about me will be true.
The New World discovered without pick or ax.

I will be what Brenda Jones was stoned for in 1969.
I saw it as a girl but didn't know I was taking in myself.

My hand remembers, treading the watery room,
just behind the rose-veiled eyes of memory.

Alone in the yard tucked beneath the hood of her car,
lucky clover all about her feet, green tea-sweet necklace
for her mud-pie crusty work boots.

She fends off their spit & words with silent two-handed
twists & turns of her socket wrench. A hurl of sticks &
stones and only me to whisper for her, from sidewalk far,

break my bones. A grown woman in grease-pocket overalls
inside her own sexy transmission despite the crowding of
hurled red hots. Beneath the hood of her candy-apple Camaro:

souped, shiny, low to the ground.

The stars over the Atlantic are dangling
salt crystals. The room at the Seashell Inn is
$20 a night; special winter off-season rate.
No one else here but us and the night clerk,
five floors below, alone with his cherished

stack of *Spiderman*. My lips are red snails
in a primal search for every constellation
hiding in the sky of your body. My hand
waits for permission, for my life to agree
to be changed, forever. Can Captain Night
Clerk hear my fingers tambourining you
there on the moon? Won't he soon climb
the stairs and *bam!* on the hood of this car?
You are a woman with film reels for eyes.
Years of long talking have brought us to the
land of the body. Our skin is one endless
prayer bead of brown. If my hand ever lands,
I will fly past dreaming Australian Aborigines.
The old claw hammer and monkey wrench
that flew at Brenda Jones will fly across the
yard of ocean at me. A grease rag will be
thrust into my painter's pants against my
will. I will never be able to wash or peel
any of this away. Before the night is over
someone I do not know will want the keys
to my '55 silver Thunderbird. He will chase
me down the street. A gaggle of spooked
hens will fly up in my grandmother's yard,
never to lay another egg, just as I am jump-
ed, kneed, pulled finally to the high ground
of sweet clover.

Nikky Finney

Miss Polly Is Akimbo underneath the Mother Emanuel Collection Table

On the occasion of swimming, with a pencil behind my ear, into
a photograph by Daniel Beltrá, Oil Spill #12, 2010

The one who came to start the next Civil War
speaks to her directly. *Have I shot you yet?*
There is no one else left to answer. In the church
basement all are dead or bleeding out. Miss Polly,
half on her knees, is askew, tilted, her last angle,

akimbo to the nine others who are sprawled and
already spiraling toward heaven. In her mind she
too is about to die. There is no place to hide when
you are the last one facing the waving gun. The air
has been invaded by a poison mix of bright red ore

spewing from his mouth. There was a spilling.
There is about to be another. He cannot see the
seeping septic colors but she can and there is no
isthmus wide enough, beneath her shield of a table,
to keep her from the current of his nonstop debris.

A floating band of iron-orange tincture crooks her
pounding heart but does not push her downstream.
She waits sideways, as high up as she can, refusing
to look at him. She knows how evil can enter through
the iris if beheld too long. She will not be all black

and blue unsure of what has been released in the
room. A river of flaming copper is moving slowly
through her blood. She is an honest woman and
has seen with her own two honest woman eyes
what hate erupting inside a man can do and what

this one has done. She decides her last words on
this earth will not be camouflaged and khaki,
handed over just before he runs out the same way
he walked in. When he shot the pastor she
could have faked it, fallen over sideways, held her-

self perfectly still, asked her body to lie for her but
that would not have been the life she has lived. It
will not be the death she dies at his feet. She turns
into the last one standing and her molten answer
arrives. It is the color of pounded beets, beaten out

of their safe skins. Her persimmon words outline
every beloved bullet-riddled body still lying on the floor.

No, you have not.

Nikky Finney

Like the Sweet Wet Earth Itself

And after sex: as after rain, a clarity that, though by now proverbial,

could still surprise. Indeed, it did surprise him. All over again,
he could feel, through and through, what most live their entire
lives merely understanding: about apology not erasing cruelty;
about forgiveness not erasing what lingers, shimmering, in cruelty's
measureless wake; about erasure not being the point, finally, one more
version of wishing backwards—which is to say,
                                             too late… The adult
cicada is not the shell-of-itself that it leaves behind. The spent casing
has nothing to do, now, with the bullet lodged in the deer's throat,
the deer long since split open, dressed, hung by hooks, to drain,
from the barn's blue rafters. Evidence is not the same
as memory. He'd forgotten, years ago, the question; but the answer—

it never left him, or hardly ever: *Yes; for the lion's foot, too, is feathered.*

Anywhere Like Peace

He's unbuttoning his shirt, we've never met before, he says
last night he had a dream about me. A good dream,
he tells me; a strong one—meaning *I* was strong, and that for the first
time in years, apparently, he felt completely safe. To confuse
closure with conclusion is nothing new, I at first
want to say to him, but a

                    shadow-softness to his face brings out
a softness in me that I don't show, usually, it makes me
want to lean hard into his chest instead, the part where the hair—
faint, still, as if still filling in—looks like two wings
positioned where they shouldn't be, but on purpose, so that
flight means for once not seeing the earth fall away, but the sky
getting steadily closer, let the body

                    approach... Will I ever
stop wanting more than what I've already got, I used to wonder,
not realizing yet that's all ambition *is*, finally; I thought
humility would be a smaller thing, a quieter
thing, it seems I was wrong about that, too. I can't
decide if it's just my being so much older now, or if it's
always been true, that winter foliage
is the prettiest foliage.

Eleven

It's the eleventh
hour on the eleventh
floor. We chose this
apartment (if not
this hour) for the light,
though my father could,
from any height, look
back. Below are oaks
and magnolias and tracks
on which freight and passenger
trains pass, and my father
knows the difference by
the blowing of their horns,
both of which he prefers,
he says, to that other one
he's hearing, by which he
means Gabriel's, disguised
as tinnitus. He's remembering also,
since it's fall, the shofar Herb
Karp blew for the new year––
a sorrowing sound, he
always said, especially if
you were a ram. That
day we moved him
from the split-
level to the eleventh
floor, we brought a few
photographs and chairs,
lamps to see the
dark with, spoons,
a cup. It was a kind
of sky burial. He
has his pocket comb.

He has his wristwatch
with the busted strap,
he has his wallet
with a dollar. He's getting
smaller and smaller, his vast
past vaster. Looking out
from the eleventh hour
is like looking from
a hole punched to make
a room into a *camera
obscura.* Anything can
be a camera. Anyone
might be in this aerie,
but today it's us, watching
on the compact TV what
he watched, rapt
at the Imperial Theatre
in 1936—Buster Crabbe
as Flash Gordon, trying
to stop the planet Mongo
from colliding with Earth.
I forget how it ends, my
father says, *but it ends.*
And then we're looking
from the small screen out
the sliding glass toward
dusk, where below us,
on fluted, Spanish roofs,
two men in straw hats
are ambling the inclines
of tiles without ropes
or harnesses, without
fear. One man is tossing
bottles of water to the other,
who's smoking a cigarette

Andrea Cohen

and catching the bottles,
and I'm thinking danger
and OSHA and laborers
in the vineyard and my
father from his eleventh
hour says—*lucky devils.*

Acapulco

He was talking about the random
axe of God, his hand slamming
the table like a battle axe, and though
I was a non-believer, I believed
(I knew) we were sitting, against all odds,
together, with nothing but a checkered
tablecloth between us, in North Bay, where
the maître d' embraced him and seemed to
want to hug me too. The man had written
to say he'd known my father would die
one day, that he'd been preparing nearly
forty years for that, since he was seventeen
and had needed a psychiatrist roughly
his father's age, Jewish, and on the right
bus line. By then, he said, his father had
been dead five years. My father, he said,
was the first person he confessed his love
of men in dark suits to. How gentle he was,
the man said. How wise. *He was the father
I didn't have,* the man said, and I thought, he
was the father I didn't have either.
The man was a public defender,
and when the waiter brought the wrong
cut of beef, he said, *everyone is innocent
of something.* We were sitting like
two people who had met in another
life and were trying to catch up. I asked
what had happened to his father and he
said *swimming* and *Acapulco.* He said
shark. And it occurred to me that we
were breaking breadsticks together because
a fish had mistaken a man for something
else. It's a big, random axe. *It Never Entered*

Andrea Cohen

My Mind was playing above and around us—
a sea of Sinatra. *That was your father's favorite,*
the man said, which surprised me, because
I always thought my father liked music
unburdened by words, the way he liked his
evenings with us. I didn't tell the man
about the app you can get now, how it tells
you where sharks are in real time. I didn't
tell him about the woman who reaches
into the mouths of hammerheads to cut
hooks out, how after she's pulled a hook
from one shark, others approach, sensing,
no, knowing, she means to help them.
That's a belief system. The world is teeming
with them, and leaving the restaurant,
the man pointed out, as men tend to,
the stars comprising Orion's Belt—
as if it were the lustrous sparks and not
the leveling dark that connects us.

Suzanne Gardinier

Mala 60 / Conerstone

1 The roof first: couldn't I just stay there,
2 on the verge, on the edge, hands over my face,
3 with the licks of flame just beginning,
4 what licks, what flame, who cares where
5 all this came from, & what's underneath: I forget
6 who built it, & how, using what for mortar,
7 & what happens next, once it starts burning:
8 that's the language people speak where I live: .

9 I forget, I don't know what you're talking about,
10 who ever heard of such a thing,
11 as the fire turns the roof into air
12 & starts to work its way down:
13 there's no way to know how it really happened,
14 you needn't always assume the worst,
15 as the fire like a scythe takes the living
16 tops of the nearmost grasses away,

17 & down, now clearing the upstairs bedrooms,
18 the night air pouring through as if it's helping
19 & if you were on the roof, now you've fallen
20 to the rooms with bells & cushions & trays,
21 with wallpaper covered in invisible fingerprints
22 the fire makes visible just before
23 pouring through like a mighty stream or something:
24 What did you think it was made of anyway:

25 If the house is a country, yes, let's say that,
26 a country house, with columns, as if
27 whoever lived here before had no
28 place to breathe between there & Athens & Rome,
29 whose burned roof transferred to a hill in Virginia,
30 a virgin house, on virgin land,

31 they're clean words, aren't they, city, country,
32 virgin, Athens, land, plantation:
33 a virgin house where generations
34 of what-should-I-call-it reproduce
35 magically, it's a magic house
36 at the summit of all human endeavor,
37 arranged in meticulous hierarchies,
38 to be studied, to be reproduced exactly
39 & over & over, for hundreds of years:
40 a plantation house with a fire pouring through

41 the bedrooms: the latifundio's privacy,
42 far from where that fire's headed,
43 what cellar, what cell, what cornerstone—
44 & how else could it have, & why must you,
45 & for now we're in the long hallway, off of which
46 the serving trays, beside the feather beds
47 & whatever else might occur to them
48 & lines of chamber pots & pallets & shoes:

49 of which the fire makes quick work, not
50 like the house work, so long you could think
51 maybe unending, until tonight,
52 every fiber of every sheet
53 making its contribution to the project
54 of recomposition, the white house made air,
55 air even, once the smoke clears,
56 the ghosts starting to gather might breathe:
57 & down, & because the fire comes at night,
58 the people upstairs are gone,
59 the sleepers, if you want to remember their faces
60 think of someone turning away from what she can't
61 stop seeing, who stops seeing,
62 & someone else walking that way
63 you walk when you leave a sickness so long
64 it becomes just the way you live—

65 until the fire comes, after your whole life
66 passes waiting for that day, that night,
67 on the first floor the salons to prevent it
68 & the footsteps of those trying to speed its day,
69 the kitchen where they dreamed about it,
70 the old ways erased the way the fire
71 is erasing the house, the way it is
72 made nature, until the fire comes:
73 in the smoke you could hang on to for a minute,
74 to the way it is almost the way it was,
75 hanging suspended, like what else, I don't want to
76 carry these ashes in my pockets anymore,
77 in my eyelashes, under my fingernails,
78 this house made of ashes always but not
79 so plain like this, as the fire
80 turns the hill house into night sky:

81 the first floor, the front door
82 where who stood & who bowed & who entered,
83 the acropolis of the Américas, what
84 gibberish is that, I can't hear what you're saying,
85 were you invited or did you arrange the flowers
86 the day someone near you passed & they were dancing
87 & you poured from the pitchers of oblivion
88 & they danced like that fire's dancing tonight:
89 purposeful, intent, improvising & patterned,
90 the front door all the way back to the kitchen,
91 & time enough to travel out, beyond the hill,
92 but tonight the work is down:
93 through the carpets & the floorboards & what did you think
94 you'd find there, no matter where you lived,
95 awake or asleep, the fire finds it,
96 past hiding : the cornerstone :

97 It looks familiar, doesn't it, if you catch
98 a glimpse before the flames get to work,

99 visible with the house almost gone
100 & the place it settled stirring underneath,
101 as the fire moves through its ancient assignment,
102 familiar even though you've never seen it
103 because you've seen it every day
104 & at night behind your closed eyes:

105 this place this fire was traveling toward
106 all this time, so one night you couldn't not see
107 where all this came from & what's underneath
108 where I come from, where I live.

Deborah A. Miranda

Offerings

At dawn the songs begin again as if never sung before,
as if the jet stream has not wandered from its path,

the Arctic ice shelf does not melt at accelerated rates,
Sudden Oak Death does not leapfrog across the continent.

Shenandoah Valley songbirds lean into the indigo air
as if two thousand snow geese did not fall from the sky

in Idaho, ten thousand sea lions are not washing up dead
in the Channel Islands, train tanker cars full of chemicals

never crashed into the Kanawah River in West Virginia.
As if California's Central Valley agriculture is not pumping

twenty-thousand-year-old water out of ancient aquifers
that cannot be refilled. These song warriors pitch morning

as if the territorial prayers of robins keep bee-colony collapse
disorder at bay, as if crows stitch each torn morning together

with their black beaks, mockingbirds know the secret
combination of notes that command God's ear, the low *coo*

of mourning doves weaves feathery medicine; they persist
as if pine warblers, flash of gold in treetops, coax the sun

up by degrees, as if these musical beings don't know the word
extinction, as if, knowing it, their silvered melodies insist

like the yellow warbler: *sweet-sweet-sweet; little-more-sweet.*

God's House

Imagine the inside of a sand dollar:
arches rising to a peaked roof, light
streaming in through tiny holes.

Turtle Woman looks for that cathedral
everywhere. Tries Assembly of God,
St. Stephen's, Temple Beth El.

Lets Mormon sisters named Betty,
Linda, and Rita show her how to fold
her arms and pray. Reads her mother's

books: *Seth Speaks, Silva Mind Control,
Jonathan Livingston Seagull.* Reads King
James, The Torah, The Gnostics.

Turtle Woman never was any good
at reading maps but she knows God's house
isn't in the hot, black-topped trailer park

where an old man in a two-tone
blue and white Chevy offers little girls
25 cents in exchange for a kiss.

Not at Vacation Bible School
in between popsicle-stick-and-yarn
God's eyes and Jesus Loves Me.

Not under the turquoise sting
of the swimming pool's beguiling
waters that nearly claim her breath.

Maybe God is homeless. Turtle Woman
wonders, is that God's blue tarp
under the trees beside the Interstate?

She imagines God hauling a rusty cart
over curbs, fighting for the last bed
at a shelter down on First Ave. Maybe

God's in line with her uncles and brother
down at the YMCA, waiting for a turn
in the shower. Maybe God just packed up,

moved on to a cheaper neighborhood.
Turtle Woman sighs: she's tired of looking.
Maybe she'll build God a tiny house,

an invitation, an altar, down on the beach
where the tide does baptisms twice daily,
and the sky is a dome full of saints.

D.A. Powell

The Pleasures of the Dark

Fear not, we are none of us born wise.
           Some are born ghosts, divided
at the threshold from an aching form we long to take
in the brown brick archways. If we aren't turned away.

           Have you been licked by the flames of geraniums
in boxes set along the edges of the streets? It does not burn.
           And if you admit me to your home—
               No, that's already too much.
I couldn't haunt your lonely abode.
           Daylight, and you'd see through me.
Daylight, and faith would cease, and one of us
would ask awkwardly to be excused
           back into the famished thoroughfare
from whence he first appeared. That's too much work.

I'm already vanishing. And you see, nervous postulant—
surely by now I thought you'd leave as well.
But shadows increase in shadow,
           a creed grows out of need,
and nobody wants to die alone in another man's bed,
when he can be taken right here on his knees.

The End of the Pride Parade

I went to the parade and watched people wave at Wells Fargo.
I watched them wave at Harvey Milk, now more than
thirty years dead, and lift up their phones. Look at me
with a drag queen, they'll scream at their kids one day. Love
has been sponsored into law but a lot of you didn't vote
for it. I did not come for the free t shirt. I came for the free
condoms that'll sit in my hopechest like a bill that keeps
getting tabled in congress. Where is the fuck brigade? I went
to the dick parade. It was the same as this but I didn't get
a lei from the US Bank. There was no Chipotle float
¿Homo Estas? with a giant foil-wrapped cylinder representing
the burrito of equality. Folks are cheering in the streets
for Walmart, whose workers have shown up pushing unironic
shopping carts. After them comes Dignity Health and Yahoo,
Orlando Strong. Then Macy's and the Berkeley free clinic.
Someone ran off with our dildo and turned it into a marketing
tool. Bring back the street heaux, bb. Don't step in the vomit.

Lure

I am not there

(We are not in that room.
I am not sitting on your lap.
I am not wearing the yellow
and white gingham skirt so pretty
Grandmother just made for me
this morning. Grandmother
is not sitting at her sewing
machine, revving the pedal hard
like an accelerator, driving herself
through the needle. You are not alive.
That fifth of whiskey is not empty
inside your pocket.

I am not three.
You are not seventy-nine.
Your fishhook fingers
are not toddling my birdseed
nipples over and over again.
I am not admiring the shine
of my new white patent leather shoes
resting at the edge of your knee.
Your other hand is not digging
inside my brand-new *Friday*
panties Aunt Lydia just gave to me
last week, because she was so proud
that instead of peeing in my diaper,
I'd learned to make it in the toilet. Grandmother
is not still sitting at her sewing maching, throttling
the pedal harder, louder. This is not your hand, your mouth
your Pall Mall fingers, your fishhooks, your pearl-

handled switchblade. My father is not at work
mopping floors, unaware of me, sitting here
inside your lap. Alligator.

I am not three. I am not
breathing. I am not sitting in
your lap forgetting the body
has feet and legs and muscle
and sinew. And breath.
I am not just staring
at the wall.

Those are not your countless splendid
black bamboo fishing rods still hanging
upright out there on the garage walls.
Those are not the five gallons of salt
water sitting so still and pale
on the kitchen floor, the ones
we collected yesterday at the beach, to help
my sister's skin. We did not climb down
onto the giant rocks. Grandmother
did not tie pretty silk scarves under our chins
to cover our hair. We did not play
Hide-and-Seek with cranky blue crabs.
That beauty of a day never happened.
There is not a two-story giant avacado tree
in your backyard, whom I love more
than life. There is no grass, no
Pacific, no New Orleans, no Mardi Gras
stories for which I long, no boxes Mamere sends
each hot winter, filled with pralines and fudge
and purple and yellow and green plastic beads.
No Hail Mary blessed art thou amongst women—
I am not here.

Robin Coste Lewis

My skin does not hurt.
My blood will not spill grey
anywhere. You will not find me
year after year. I will not ever remember
a thing. I will not stare at walls.
I will not see you, all my life, peering
at me from around random corners, whispering
something delicious out of a lover's mouth.

I will not dislike the feeling of touch, will not
be repulsed by the look of desire in an eye.
I will not allow my teeth to rot. The metal
implements of the dentist will not smell
sharp like fresh shucked pearls.

They did not send my mother away
when she was a little girl. They did not
put her on a Jim Crow train alone, in the middle
of a war, headed for Chicago, to make sure
you'd never touch her again, and again, for years.
You did not ever touch her again. They did not
not kill you. Again and again. They did not
not slice your body into fine brilliant offerings.

This is not that feeling that this is my body,
but I am somehow trapped inside
another girl, unable to say or feel a thing.
This is not the memory of another day.
I am not a wet headless footless squirming
thing you dug up from the dirt beneath the red
anthurium next to Grandmother's breathy
greenhouse and twisted onto a hook. I am not
a fresh pink pulsing thing splayed
on a tray my mother leaves
on your front porch

every Friday, dressed
so pretty. Violet. Hibiscus.
Red Bird. Of Paradise.
I am not there.
The air is not
frozen)

any longer.

The Body in August

Because when I was a child, God would pull me up into Her lap. Because when She pulled me up into Her lap, She would read to me. Because the story She read most was the one I liked least. Because every day She'd open that thin green book and say, This is the story of your life. Because, from beginning to end, there were only three pages.

I believe in that road that is infinite and black and goes on blindly forever. I believe crocodiles swallow rocks to help them digest crab. Because up until the twentieth century, people could still die from sensation. And because my hunger is so deep, I am ashamed to lift my head.

Because memory—not gravity—pins us to this trembling. And when God first laid eyes on us, She went mad from envy. Because if the planet had a back door, we'd all still be there—waiting for the air to approve our entry. Because your eyes were the only time the peonies said yes to me. Because no matter how many times I died, I always woke up again—happy.

Then, last night, after I'd yelled at him for the first time, my new son dreamt we went walking inside the trees. When we came across a squirrel, he said, I'd kicked it. Then the squirrel changed into a thin green book, which we read.

Because when God became a small child, I pulled Her up into my lap. Because when I pulled Her into my lap—to please her—I opened my blouse. Because Her mouth is an impossibly pink place, a gaping raw cathedral, which She opened, teeth-to-nipple, then clamped down.

Lisa Dordal

Love Poem

I love how the words
My Mother and I

are like a door, slightly open,
the darkness itself

peeking out.
I love the hunger

of a baby bird
showing its red infinity

to the world. I love
three kinds of consciousness—

flesh, ghost, divine.
I love the blue vein

beneath the skin
of my right wrist—

how it forgave me
immediately.

Broken Arm

Like you hold a baby, the nurse said. *Hold your arm*
like you hold a baby. And I held it that way.

My fingers fat with pain I couldn't feel
as I breathed *come back* onto my suddenly strange skin.

Like you hold a baby.

We had a son once. For a week calling him Ben.
A name the birth mother loved. And we loved

the way she said his name. Until she changed her mind
and the future became a house we weren't permitted to enter,

and the future became a great homesickness.
Which is how some traditions refer to the divine.

Which is to say everywhere and nowhere,
like salt dissolved in water. And now there is a boy

with a voice we can't hear, and a boy with a voice
we can't un-hear. A boy who might love darkness,

might love searching for constellations—
new ones that he can name. A boy

who makes dinosaurs from blue clay, each one
with three hearts. *You can't see them but they're there.*

Ben, the birth mother said. *Like you hold a baby,*
the nurse said. Like a great homesickness

that might be god, or might be grief.

John Keene

Mission and Outpost

in memory of C. L. Hillyer

Beneath the awning of the Leland no one
passes as I saunter, hungrily, rolling
from ball to heel on my not-sore foot, waiting,
eyes keyed for anybody trolling

or trying to. No luck; just this drizzly mausoleum,
where I had imagined a western Oz,
an emerald knob of pastel-gabled Victorians
exulting beneath a pearly vault of sky, whose

beauty, sublimity, should serve as sign and seal
of my redemption. Instead, gray, gummy hills
of concrete, dank, steep oily inclines that only wind
me towards dizziness. No sun as rain spirals

into iridescent eddies at the curb: the TV claimed
that silvery storm-rivers were on tomorrow's bill. Across the fray
hustlers ply the bars, play tiddlywinks with johns.
This side, a runaway, a drag junkie, though Polk is hardly the gay

hub it once was; that eminence still clings to the Castro.
I turn and you pull up. Now as we zoom
there, climbing, dipping on Market I recall the many books,
the magazines I'd scoured in that tomb

deep under Cambridge, how I'd combed and cleared
the HQ section, hoping to unearth and use like Dedalus
that perfect thread of information that would guide me
from my labyrinth, grow wise, salvage and loose

the sybarite trapped inside. Instead what I found were tips
on how to dress, pack my cock, achieve the ultimate in clone
perfection; how to cruise and lay and lose the gold-tressed,
virile god of every queer boy's fantasies—but mine; bemoan

the arrival of one's sexual autumn, the dying light
of the Pines or dunes of Provincetown; work a bathhouse or four—
and where they hunkered in every civilized metropole; popper,
coke and fist my way to true liberation; keep score

by counting the number of times you'd hit the clinic, beat it, got it
again, forgotten and passed it on again; and then more tales
about young, tanned, muscular vapid beauties who'd disappeared
or gone mad or both; and all those grand parades, processions, festivals–

stocked with garish, compelling "types"—all beginning
and ending *here*. Instead, no confirmation
tonight of memory's emulsion: only flashes of men I've known,
a rangy afro'd brother, a thickset guy, Asian,

in a bomber, a cordillera of *chicos*, buff and bundled,
dishing in quiet tones, switching by. As by plan we dine
before your tour at Ma Tante Sumi; all about us the ravage
remains invisible. A surviving link in the chain

you become the evening's griot, pointing out where what once was
is or isn't or will be or would have been, what gave
in '70, '74, '80, expatiate about the reefery bliss that wafted up
to the marquee of the Castro Theater, how each wave,

native, arrivant, transformed this beachhead of *yerba buena*
into his or her own paradise, figured out what really
mattered were the deepest exigencies of pleasure, the soul's
satisfaction. One perceives it here, despite the steely,

spitty air, this district's slow contraction. Before the glowing panes,
I peer in, wired by the meal, the wine, a tyro feeling veteran,
awed and so jejune, as though this were unreal, I'd seen it all
before. Tiring swiftly, you say goodbye, drive off, as a red-faced man

accosts me, drags me to meet his "friends": a ratty white
twentysomething; a boohooing queen; a faun-haired boy
soon to turn his tail in porn to pay his rent. I hand over coins,
slip away, idling pensively in the downpour, coy

to inscrutability. I mean to retrace our circuit and do, begin
again, take stock, envision myself on this date
in this same spot twenty years before, but falter halfway
through: my imagination sags beneath the weight

of disappointment on this shadow trail; I halt, regroup, reel
in my stories, but fail, for I'm lost and can't divine
even the few strong clues you've left me, while
a ponytailed stud stares uneasily, as if observing the blind.

And so I follow my steps backwards, to the Jaguar's shelves
of tchotchkes, in A Different Light I browse, dry
off, then slip into the Pendulum for a sip of beer.
It's midnight: my head leaden as I hum along and sigh,

admiring the leathered and rubber-clad legions
prowling, chatting, renewing the Castro's rites,
my yearning this snapshot before joining them,
as the hills bloom with stars and headlights.

Intimacy

If my mother were
alive, she'd want to

know how it was

my husband and I
met, would want to

know what it meant

to hookup on
dating sites, what

exactly an "ass-

hungry power top
with a dick that won't

quit" looks like, and I

would have to do
my best to tell her

exactly what I was

looking for because
that's what intimacy

is all about, having

spent a few decades
flat on my back

on a couch in a room

papered over in neutral
colors, testing out

my faith in a talking

cure as I got all
gussied up for my

meet-cute that would

outlast the years
my mother had left

on this earth, the deck

she kept on shuffling
right up to the end

a bit worn-out but

complete were it not
for all the Kings

that went missing—

Thoreau

My father and I have no place to go.
His wife will not let us in the house—
afraid of catching AIDS. She thinks
sleeping with men is more than a sin,
my father says, as we sit on the curb
in front of someone else's house.
Sixty-four years have made my father
impotent. Silver roots, faded black
dye mottling his hair make him look
almost comical, as if his shame
belonged to me. Last night we read
Thoreau in a steak house down the road
and wept: *If a man does not keep pace*
with his companions, let him travel
to the music that he hears, however
measured or far away. The orchards
are gone, his village near Shanghai
bombed by the Japanese, the groves
I have known in Almaden—apricot,
walnut, peach and plum—hacked down.

Rest Stop, Highway 91

        Cars parked alongside a chain-link fence
overlooking houses that have no view,
       plates from three bordering states aglow
           in the light from a hillside billboard
     filled with a glass of milk—Holyoke
just beyond the notch, slumbering
       like a rain-soaked paper on the porch—
          checkout boys from the local A&P
     hanging up their aprons, clocking out
on a night that is young only once
       in a stranger's car—the taste of skin
          on clandestine tongues, freckled swirls
     down creamy backs in constellations
left unnamed, stiff cocks under boxers
       crammed into that vinyl dark perfumed
          by a four-inch cardboard pine dangling
     above the illuminated dash, windows veiled
with frost. They say the leaves will fall
       earlier this year, like so many apples
          plastered on the hill, wooden barrels
     filling up with rain while children turn
in their sleep—deaf to the sound of engines
       running, their fathers behind the wheel.

hulk smash

because it was afternoon
and I was at the carnation farm
when the earthquake struck

because by the time I arrived
back home to help my family
traffic jams had clogged shut
the main arterial roads leading
inland from Futaba-machi

because when the tsunami
breached the sea wall,
and concrete disintegrated like
strewn chunks of soggy plywood,
we had to leave our car
and flee for higher ground

because the elevated hill
marked as the evacuation point
for an elementary school
seemed like it should be safe,
until the tsunami rose like
a thundering wall of water
and blotted out the sky

because there wasn't time
for us to climb all the way
up the hill, so I held my wife
and daughter in my arms,
and we clung together tightly
wrapped around a tree

because the icy water
uprooted the tree so easily,
like plucking up a blade
of grass, and tore my wife
Mayumi away from me

because I could see Natsu
was crying for her mother,
though I couldn't hear her

above the roar of the water,
and I was scared I'd hurt her
from holding on so tight

because when I regained
consciousness again with
a concussion and a broken leg
after having blacked out,
my arms were empty

because she was only three

because I was taken against
my will to a hospital in Iitate,
where I was promised that
rescue workers would search
the coast for any survivors
and bring them to safety

because the meltdowns
and hydrogen explosions
at Fukushima Daiichi began
the next day and everyone
within a 20-kilometer radius
was evacuated, so that
no one was able to look for
my wife or my daughter

Lee Ann Roripaugh

because the nuclear accident
at Fukushima Daiichi was,
as it turns out, preventable

because what if my wife
and daughter were injured,
but still alive, and what if
someone had only searched
for them during those early
days after the tsunami?

because it was over a month
before I was allowed back
into the exclusion zone,
where I found Mayumi's
body in a nearby rice field

because my wife's remains
were so terribly decomposed
after having been left out
to weather the elements, insects,
birds, and vermin, she was
no longer recognizable,
and the Buddhist burial rites
could not be followed
before her body was burned

because over four years
have passed with my life still
in limbo, unable to return
to what's left of my home,
to my work breeding carnations,
unable to lay Mayumi's ashes
to rest on ancestral grounds

because my daughter Natsu
is still missing, even though
I search for her every month
in the five-hour increments
allowed by radiation guidelines

because I am by nature
a quiet and scientific man,
a botanist by trade, but
I work so ferociously at
clearing debris and digging
along the shoreline in search
of my daughter's remains—
tearing off my hazmat gear
when it gets in the way,
or when it becomes too hot—
that volunteer search teams
have nicknamed me The Hulk

because so what, I no longer
care about being exposed
to radiation, and maybe
it'll make me stronger anyway,
like the weird profusion
of too-bright and hardy flowers
blooming in the irradiated wake
of Hiroshima and Nagasaki...
maybe even strong enough
to hold on to what matters.

because plans are underway
to build a containment facility
in Futaba City for the bags
upon bags of contaminated topsoil
and radioactive debris gathered
by the cleanup workers that
no one knows what to do with

because if this happens
Futaba will become just
a permanent trash site
for nuclear waste, a toxic
garbage dump, where
my daughter's remains
will be abandoned forever

because how can I let this be?

because my arms are empty

because she was only three

because now, every month
when I spend my five hours
searching the no go zone,
and I see one of the many
rusted TEPCO signs reading
*Nuclear Power: Bright Future
of Energy,* I feel such a huge
surge of adrenaline and rage,
that I have to tear it down

CAConrad

from *Listen to the Golden Boomerang Return*

swallowed
each other
until we
heard
each
other
think
queer pirates
I have loved
loosened my
wilderness
no
more
miscounting
butterflies in
our utopia
let's make
poems
that
can
rob
a bank

losing
  something
    too important
          to lose
          is hard
          the first
          time so
          next time
    ransom April's song
    before it finds itself
I took my time finding
      the right man to
      build this wall
        against the
        phantasm
          we're rowing to
          the middle of
          the Bermuda
      Triangle we
      send our
      love

Richard Siken

Boot Theory

A man walks into a bar and says:
                    Take my wife—please.
                                        So you do.
        You take her out into the rain and you fall in love with her
                            and she leaves you and you're desolate.
    You're on your back in your undershirt, a broken man
            on an ugly bedspread, staring at the water stains
                                            on the ceiling.
            And you can hear the man in the apartment above you
                        taking off his shoes.
    You hear the first boot hit the floor and you're looking up,
                                    you're waiting
        because you thought it would follow, you thought there would be
            some logic, perhaps, something to pull it all together
        but here we are in the weeds again,
                                here we are
    in the bowels of the thing: your world doesn't make sense.
            And then the second boot falls.
                            And then a third, a fourth, a fifth.

    A man walks into a bar and says:
                    Take my wife—please.
                            But you take him instead.
    You take him home, and you make him a cheese sandwich,
            and you try to get his shoes off, but he kicks you
                                and he keeps kicking you.
        You swallow a bottle of sleeping pills but they don't work.
            Boots continue to fall to the floor
                            in the apartment above you.
    You go to work the next day pretending nothing happened.
            Your co-workers ask
                        if everything's okay and you tell them

you're just tired.
And you're trying to smile. And they're trying to smile.

A man walks into a bar, you this time, and says:
                    Make it a double.
        A man walks into a bar, you this time, and says:
                                    Walk a mile in my shoes.
A man walks into a convenience store, still you, saying:
            I only wanted something simple, something generic...
    But the clerk tells you to buy something or get out.
A man takes his sadness down to the river and throws it in the river
            but then he's still left
with the river. A man takes his sadness and throws it away
                            but then he's still left with his hands.

A Primer for the Small Weird Loves

1

The blond boy in the red trunks is holding your head underwater
because he is trying to kill you,
    and you deserve it, you do, and you know this,
        and you are ready to die in this swimming pool
because you wanted to touch his hands and lips and this means
            your life is over anyway.
    You're in the eighth grade. You know these things.
You know how to ride a dirt bike, and you know how to do
    long division,
and you know that a boy who likes boys is a dead boy, unless
        he keeps his mouth shut, which is what you
            didn't do,
because you are weak and hollow and it doesn't matter anymore.

2

A dark-haired man in a rented bungalow is licking the whiskey
from the back of your wrist.
    He feels nothing,
      keeps a knife in his pocket,
           peels an apple right in front of you
    while you tramp around a mustard-colored room
in your underwear
        drinking Dutch beer from a green bottle.
    After everything that was going to happen has happened
you ask only for the cab fare home
      and realize you should have asked for more
          because he couldn't care less, either way.

3

The man on top of you is teaching you how to hate, sees you
as a piece of real estate,
                    just another fallow field lying underneath him
                              like a sacrifice.
He's turning your back into a table so he doesn't have to
          eat off the floor, so he can get comfortable,
pressing against you until he fits, until he's made a place for himself
                                        inside you.
The clock ticks from five to six. Kissing degenerates into biting.
     So you get a kidney punch, a little blood in your urine.
                    It isn't over yet, it's just begun.

4

Says to himself
          The boy's no good. The boy is just no good.
     but he takes you in his arms and pushes your flesh around
                    to see if you could ever be ugly to him.
You, the now familiar whipping boy, but you're beautiful,
                              he can feel the dogs licking his heart.
     Who gets the whip and who gets the hoops of flame?
                    He hits you and he hits you and he hits you.
Desire driving his hands right into your body.
          Hush, my sweet. These tornadoes are for you.
You wanted to think of yourself as someone who did these kinds of things.
          You wanted to be in love
                    and he happened to get in the way.

5

The green-eyed boy in the powder-blue t-shirt standing
next to you in the supermarket recoils as if hit,
          repeatedly, by a lot of men, as if he has a history of it.
This is not your problem.

You have your own body to deal with.
The lamp by the bed is broken.
You are feeling things he's no longer in touch with.
And everyone is speaking softly,
so as not to wake one another.
The wind knocks the heads of the flowers together.
Steam rises from every cup at every table at once.
Things happen all the time, things happen every minute
that have nothing to do with us.

6

So you say you want a deathbed scene, the knowledge that comes
before knowledge,
and you want it dirty.
And no one can ever figure out what you want,
and you won't tell them,
and you realize the one person in the world who loves you
isn't the one you thought it would be,
and you don't trust him to love you in a way
you would enjoy.
And the boy who loves you the wrong way is filthy.
And the boy who loves you the wrong way keeps weakening.
You thought if you handed over your body
he'd do something interesting.

7

The stranger says there are no more couches and he will have to
sleep in your bed. You try to warn him, you tell him
you will want to get inside him, and ruin him,
but he doesn't listen.
You do this, you do. You take the things you love
and tear them apart
or you pin them down with your body and pretend they're yours.
So, you kiss him, and he doesn't move, he doesn't

pull away, and you keep on kissing him. And he hasn't moved,
he's frozen, and you've kissed him, and he'll never
                    forgive you, and maybe now he'll leave you alone.

Richard Blanco

Love as if Love

Before I dared kiss a man, I kissed
Elizabeth. Before I was a man, I was
twenty-three and she was thirty-five,
a woman old enough to know songs
I didn't—and that we wouldn't last
beyond the six weeks spent drinking
sweet German wine off our lips,
candles burning and music lifting
off the black vinyl, easing the taboo
between us, barefoot and sprawled
on blankets over her studio floor.

She played The Mamas & The Papas,
Holiday, and Carole King, closed my eyes
with her fingers until the notes broke
in my palms and the room filled up
with the flicker of monarchs. She sang
her life to me in lyrics about running
like a river, about rain, fire. She sang
until I wasn't afraid of her loose hair,
the scent of lilacs creased in her neck,
her small bones in the space between
her breasts, until I dared undress her.

Before I ever took a man, I gave in
to Elizabeth by the tiny green lights
of her stereo glowing like fireflies,
the turntable a shiny black moon
spinning with the songs I still hear
on the radio—driving and singing
straight into clouds moving farther
and farther away, but never quite
vanishing, like those nights falling
asleep with her rooted in my arms,
loving her as if I could love her.

Maybe

for Craig

Maybe it was the billboards promising
paradise, maybe those fifty-nine miles
with your hand in mine, maybe my sexy
roadster, the top down, maybe the wind
fingering your hair, sun on your thighs
and bare chest, maybe it was just the ride
over the sea split in two by the highway
to Key Largo, or the idea of Key Largo.
Maybe I was finally in the right place
at the right time with the right person.
Maybe there'd finally be a house, a dog
named Chu, a lawn to mow, neighbors,
dinner parties, and you forever obsessed
with crossword puzzles and Carl Jung,
reading in the dark by the moonlight,
at my bedside every night. Maybe. Maybe
it was the clouds paused at the horizon,
the blinding fields of golden sawgrass,
the mangrove islands tangled, inseparable
as we might be. Maybe I should've said
something, promised you something,
asked you to stay a while, maybe.

Mark Bibbins

from *13th Balloon*

Scraps of magazines
hoarded by boys
in our fort in the woods
The pictures were what   nude women
cavorting in a gym
nude women lying on a tile floor

I told myself not to look
at the boy next to me
in the horny grim leaflight
as he studied page after seedy page
I told myself   don't wish
for us to be nude together now
nude in the branches   nude in the clouds

Don't look at the other boy
in case he sees me looking at him
      Look down at the dead leaves
on which are projected
nude photos of me   nude photos of him
nude photos of him all slippery with me

Don't look for the two
of us nude on the rocks
where the sunlight cuts through
       the two of us
nude at the edge of the stream

Don't look at him   don't look
don't look at his hand   at his crotch
better to look at the ground instead

///

What is it they say about water
something about it seeking itself
and how did jokes like this one move
so quickly through the world in 1983

What's the hardest thing about having AIDS
Convincing your parents you're Haitian

Did they spew out of fax machines
were they blurted over happy-hour beers
by somebody's uncle
who worked for the state   or by another's
brother who worked in a garage
their jokes attaching themselves like leeches
to the swollen host of suffering
        ugly but not useless
in order that we might endure
whatever side of suffering we're on

What does GAY stand for
Got AIDS Yet

How many other acronyms crossed the membrane
that separated my rural high school
from the rest of the world and entered
the gym one afternoon
filling it like a syringe   Which boys
among us had just been watching
our friends in the showers
        imagining their bodies
        sliding against our own
        like water seeking our own water
Which boys then saw the word AIDS
on the blood-filled test tube
on the cover of Newsweek

while other boys hooted and passed
the magazine around the locker room

Its own level   that's what water seeks
and which of these boys
was it only me   which of us
among any of these boys thought
now I know   now I know how
I'm going to die

///

Mark Wunderlich

Invention

Ghost, I have searched theaters of the flesh
for your imagined face, found you

among the boy whores working the carpeted hallways
of the cinema, or at the beach in late summer

your tanned thighs slipping from a sarong, urging me to compare you
to the heraldic figures.

My sweet invented one, I have loved you
more cleanly and with greater cruelty

than any actual suitor, to whom
I offered questions,

fed breakfast, or drove home.
I wander the empty house (memory).

You appear to me stock-still
in the snow-covered corn, guarding

what I have inflicted upon you—you.
I beg your forgiveness. I who invented you

brought you here to illustrate
my own sense of having once been shattered,

then destroyed you to show the world
I intended to be whole.

A Husband's Prayer

You, author of all wonders,
shown to us by your many prophets

and instruments—our own shoemaker's daughter,
illiterate and bent, who proclaims from her special chair

in the meetinghouse, who reminds us to be humble,
and not aspire above our station,

to find beauty in utility, and to beware idolatry—
you who chose to provide me with a spouse,

and a house, a barn and sheds, gardens,
a small orchard, a field rich with clover,

hives humid and speckled with pollen,
and who finds the greatest satisfaction

when we attend to three responsibilities:
to be a brother to another, to be a good

and kindly neighbor, to move through the world
with a mate; give me strength.

From the coolest and boggiest portion
of my heart, my worries multiply as spores

canker the apple leaf. My mate,
though weak, is there to help me

set aside my burdens, if only I could
describe them into the space between our pillows

at night. When thistles spring up in the field
of our marriage, when the noxious vine

twines onto the maple, let us pull it up
by its roots. When I gaze upon the gothic script

tattooed on the young gardener's brown stomach,
strain to read it as it folds, remind me

my own name is written in the mind of another
however faint.

Let that be enough. Let me not dwell
on our weaknesses, on our smells, our shedding

skin and hair. There is a small chalet
somewhere on the cool green pasture

of an alp where we shelter, our heads
on the striped ticking, our hands

barely touching as we sleep.

Rick Barot

Whitman, 1841

I don't know if he did or did not touch the boy.
But that boy told a brother or a father or a friend,
who told someone in a tavern, or told someone

about it while the men hauled in the nets of fish
from the Sound. Or maybe it was told to someone
on the street, a group of men talking outside

the village schoolhouse, where he was the teacher.
What was whispered about him brought everyone
to church that Sunday, where the preacher roared

his name and the pews cleared out to find him.
He was twenty-one, thought of himself as an exile.
He was boarding with the boy and his family.

The boy was a boy in that schoolroom he hated.
Not finding him in the first house, they found him
in another and dragged him from under the bed

where he had been hiding. He was led outside.
And they took the tar they used for their boats,
and they broke some pillows for their feathers,

and the biography talks about those winter months
when there was not a trace of him, until the trail
of letters, articles, stories, and poems started

up again, showing he was back in the big city.
He was done teaching. That was one part
of himself completed, though the self would never

be final, the way his one book of poems would
never stop taking everything into itself. The look
of the streets and the buildings. The look of men

and women. The names of ferry boats and trains.
The name of the village, which was Southold.
The name of the preacher, which was Smith.

On Gardens

When I read about the garden
designed to bloom only white flowers,
I think about the Spanish friar who saw one
of my grandmothers, two hundred years
removed, and fucked her. If you look
at the word *colony* far enough, you see it
traveling back to the Latin
of *inhabit*, *till*, and *cultivate*. Words

that would have meant something
to the friar, walking among the village girls
as though in a field of flowers, knowing
that fucking was one way of having
a foreign policy. As I write this, there's snow
falling, which means that every
angry thought is as short-lived as a match.
The night is its own white garden:

snow on the fence, snow on the tree
stump, snow on the azalea bushes,
their leaves hanging down like green
bats from the branches. I know it's not fair
to see qualities of injustice in the aesthetics
of a garden, but somewhere between
what the eye sees and what the mind thinks
is the world, landscapes mangled

into sentences, one color read into rage.
When the neighbors complained
the roots of our cypress were buckling
their lot, my landlord cut the tree down.
I didn't know a living thing three stories high

could be so silent, until it was gone.
Suddenly that sky. Suddenly all the light
in the windows, as though every sheet

of glass was having a migraine.
When I think about that grandmother
whose name I don't even know, I think of
what it would mean to make a garden
that blooms black: peonies and gladiolas
of deepest purple, tulips like ravens.
Or a garden that doesn't bloom at all: rocks
placed on a plane of raked gravel,

the stray leaves cleared away every hour.
If you look at the word *garden*
deep enough, you see it blossoming
in an enclosure meant to keep out history
and disorder. Like the neighbors wanting
to keep the cypress out. Like the monks
arranging the stones into an image
of serenity. When the snow stops, I walk to see

the quiet that has colonized everything.
The main street is asleep, except for the bus
that goes by, bright as a cruise ship.
There are sheet-cakes of snow on top
of cars. In front of houses, each lawn
is as clean as paper, except where the first cat
or raccoon has walked across, each track
like a barbed-wire sash on a white gown.

Caridad Moro-Gronlier

Entry

Tortillera, n.

Pronounciation: **Spanish** /tor-ti-lle-ra/, Spain, Latin, Central and South America, U.S.
Forms: Torti, Torta, Tort, Tortilla
Etymology: <Latin *tortus* (twisted), <Spanish *torta*, <German *que*, <English *queer*. Compare French *tortille*.
Origin: From term *torticera* (*tortious*), derived from Latin *tortus*, with the meaning of crooked, twisted, etc.; *torticera*, a highbrow word, by a process of popular etymology pronounced wrongly as *tortillera* by their phonetic similarity, as in "*she is tortillera*" instead of "*she is torticera*" by an error in pronunciation.

Synonyms: *amaricada, arepera, bollera, bollo, buchona, cachapera, cambuja, camionera, come coños, desviada, ententida, fricatriz, hombruna, invertida, juega tenis, kiki, lechuga, lela, lencha, lesbiana, machorra, marimacha(o), obvia, sáfica, sopaipilla, tijeras, tribada, trola, troquera, virago, webiá, zapatona*

1.
a. Homosexual woman; lesbian.
I outed myself as a tortillera at Noche Buena dinner last Christmas, and I was roasted along with the lechón.

b. Transatlantic traveler term known to connect homosexuality with the beginning of homophobia; refutes all sexual and onomatopoeic explanations (i.e., the supposed equivalency between the clapping sound made from kneading corn pancakes to the sound made during lesbian sex) as seen through the consideration of homosexual behavior as something twisted, deviant, first referenced in 1830 in the Spanish-French dictionary by M. Nuñez de Taboada, published in Madrid, in which the French word *tribade* is translated as *tortillera* and defined as "a woman who abuses another."

*My mother did not allow me to play softball in high school because the
coach was a tortillera, and she didn't want me to end up a tortillera, too.*

c. Derogatory slang that denotes deviant, twisted behavior, the
lowest form of female debasement, term known to induce emotional
distress, such as shame and self-loathing, as well as physical
symptoms including, but not limited to, anorexia, bulimia, cutting,
dermatitis, depression, enuresis, flushing, gastritis, heart palpitations,
hyperhidrosis, insomnia, irritable bowel syndrome, kyphosis, lethargy,
malaise, mania, nausea, nightmares, OCD, panic attack, paranoia,
rash, rosacea, scarring, sleepwalking, stuttering, tachycardia, tongue
biting, teeth gnashing, thinning hair, ulcers, vomiting, xerostomia.
Better my daughter be dead than a disgusting tortillera.

2. Female producer and seller of maize pancakes.
*According to Adolfo Sanchez Vazquez, upon the arrival of Spaniards
exiled to Mexico due to the Civil War, some were greeted by a sign that
read "El sindicato de Tortilleras les da la bienvenida!," which caused
someone to quip, "This is a very cosmopolitan country if even tortilleras
have a union!"*

Pulse: A Memorial in Driftwood, Cannon Beach, Oregon

We have crossed a continent
to cast forty-nine names into the sea
cuarenta y nueve nombres mangled
by anchormen—Flores, Paniagua, Sanfeliz—
on a beach strewn with the bones of giants:
Redwood, Sequoia, Sitka Spruce.
Behemoths that would not stay buried.

Before the ruined beauty of this necropolis
saplings cleaved to elders, grew
stronger in each other's arms
as they danced in darkened groves,
lit by the strobe of sunlight, dappled
limbs akimbo, unprepared for annihilation,
unprepared for the spilled sap, the glint
of the axe, the buzz saw, the prayers
planted at the root of their destruction.

I step over titans battered down
to driftwood, stripped of tannin and pulp,
bark bleached white as sheets and offer
forty-nine names to the sea
cuarenta y nueve nombres al mar.

Here I can believe the ocean
returns what she is given.

Caridad Moro-Gronlier

Maelstrom

Wind shook the trees and rain crackled
at the windows. Could it have been
any other way? Rain coming down,
clothes wet, water dripping from our hair?

At the window, could it have been
a ghost singing its final warning?
Clothes wet, water dripping from our hair,
he fell on me like rain. I could not speak.

A ghost sang its final warning
like a storm. He tore my shirt open
and fell on me like rain. I could not speak,
and I closed my eyes. It started like this.

Like a storm, he tore my shirt open,
the light in the stairwell flickering
as I closed my eyes. It started like this:
the steps pressing into my back,

the light in the stairwell flickering
sensing storm, our hands trembling.
The steps pressed into my back
under the sound of belts unbuckling.

Sensing storm, our hands trembled.
I could not watch, could not speak.
Under the sound of belts unbuckling,
a future unraveled like spun gold.

I could not watch, could not speak
then. And now, years later, the same
future unravels like spun gold:
the arguments, the body's betrayals.

Then and now, years later, the same
quiet lying about the house.
The arguments, the body's betrayals
resist closure or the quick dismissal.

This quiet lies about my house.
Again wind shakes the trees and rain crackles.
You resist closure or the quick dismissal.
Rain coming down. It started like this.

C. Dale Young

Night Air

"If God is Art, then what do we make
of Jasper Johns?" One never knows
what sort of question a patient will pose,

or how exactly one should answer.
Outside the window, snow on snow
began to answer the ground below

with nothing more than foolish questions.
We were no different. I asked again:
"Professor, have we eased the pain?"

Eventually, he'd answer me with:
"Tell me, young man, whom do you love?"
"E," I'd say, "None of the Above,"

and laugh for lack of something more
to add. For days he had played that game,
and day after day I avoided your name

by instinct. I never told him how
we often wear each other's clothes—
we aren't what many presuppose.

Call it an act of omission, my love.
Tonight, while walking to the car,
I said your name to the evening star,

clearly pronouncing the syllables
to see your name dissipate
in the air, evaporate.

Only the night air carries your words
up to the dead (the ancients wrote):
I watched them rise, become remote.

Brenda Shaughnessy

Straight's the New Gay

Because if you are a woman you should fall for another
at least once in your life

unless you are in that deviant minority of women
claiming to be 110 percent heterosexual.

In that case it is an imperative: defy your nature.
Get rid of that too-protesty 10 percent.

You, more so than normal women, will fall harder
than you ever imagined.

Your bruises will be museum-quality Ming Dynasty
frog-blossoms uprooting your veins.

Words like *penis-substitute* or *lifestyle,*
as applied to yours,

will wound and incite you into daily little wars.
This is a regime change.

Nevertheless, still a regime. You will be gayer
than the most-aborted genes,

more lesbian than anything else you will ever be.
In this way you are erased

(you've known it and feared it all along) from science,
discourse, your careers.

This is how we do it to you: we keep you extremes
to either side

and parade down the middle while you cheer us on.

I'm Over the Moon

I don't like what the moon is supposed to do.
Confuse me, ovulate me,

spoon-feed me longing. A kind of ancient
date-rape drug. So I'll howl at you, moon,

I'm angry. I'll take back the night. Using me to
swoon at your questionable light,

you had me chasing you,
the world's worst lover, over and over

hoping for a mirror, a whisper, insight.
But you disappear for nights on end

with all my erotic mysteries
and my entire unconscious mind.

How long do I try to get water from a stone?
It's like having a bad boyfriend in a good band.

Better off alone. I'm going to write hard
and fast into you moon, face-fucking.

Something you wouldn't understand.
You with no swampy sexual

promise but what we glue onto you.
That's not real. You have no begging

cunt. No panties ripped off and the crotch
sucked. No lacerating spasms

sending electrical sparks through the toes.
Stars have those.

What do you have? You're a tool, moon.
Now, noon. There's a hero.

The obvious sun, no bullshit, the enemy
of poets and lovers, sleepers and creatures.

But my lovers have never been able to read
my mind. I've had to learn to be direct.

It's hard to learn that, hard to do.
The sun is worth ten of you.

You don't hold a candle
to that complexity, that solid craze.

Like an animal carcass on the road at night,
picked at by crows,

haunting walkers and drivers. Your face
regularly sliced up by the moving

frames of car windows. Your light is drawn,
quartered, your dreams are stolen.

You change shape and turn away,
letting night solve all night's problems alone.

Brenda Shaughnessy

Rigoberto González

from "The Bordercrosser's Pillowbook"

things that shine in the night

Fulgencio's silver crown—when he snores
the moon, coin of Judas, glaring
at the smaller metals we call stars
my buckle
the tips of my boots
the stones in my kidneys
an earring
a tear on the cheek
the forked paths of a zipper
the blade of the pocketknife triggering open
the blade of the pocketknife seducing the orange
the blade of the pocketknife salivating
the blade of the pocketknife
the word México
the word migra

things that open like flowers in daylight

Fulgencio's eyes
Fulgencio's mouth—as he yawns
the buttons on his shirt
the orange peel—the campsite—the desert—the world
the jacaranda behind the house
the roof—the clothesline—the curtains
the door that swells in the heat
the pipes that shrink in the cold
the couch—the table—the lamp
the dominoes
the dishes
the children—the wife—the neighbors
memory
the white sparks in my brain
the red sparks in my heart
the stones in my kidneys

Rigoberto González

things I would say to Fulgencio if I could say them

erase our shadows
carve our names in stone
let us watch for comets while we rest
let us not make wishes that will not come true
your shoes abandoned you the way I never will
let me fan the fires on your toes
these are the final drops of my fear—drink them
these are the final drops of my fever—drink them
these are the final drops of my love—drink them
hold me—I have a flame on my tongue
hold me—you are a mouth of water
hold me—we taste of tangerines
hold me

Carmen Giménez

from *Be Recorder*

prose v poetry
poetry v nation-state
nation-state v my hoard
my hoard v the dog
the dog v the scorpion
the scorpion v dirt
dirt v lamictal
lamictal v ennui
ennui v blunder
blunder v debt
debt v defect
defect v fucking
fucking v instagram
instagram v art
art v weed
weed v night
night v the wimpy kid
the wimpy kid v disquisition
disquisition v testing
testing v parallelism
parallelism v your textual surface
your textual surface v a glare
a glare v balm
balm v heat
heat v talking
talking v getting
getting v the diurnal clock
the diurnal clock v semester
semester v my tender spirit
my tender spirit v twaddle
twaddle v our wreckage
our wreckage v diagnosis
diagnosis v committee
committee v postfeminism

postfeminism v perimenopause
perimenopause v sentimentality
sentimentality v television
television v us
us v apple
apple v family
family v flight
flight v the bourgeoisie
the bourgeoisie v torpor
torpor v sunshine
sunshine v your company
your company v my duplicity
my duplicity v your ease
your ease v my programming
my programming v your door
your door v my puddles
my puddles v progeny
progeny v prose

•

I became American each time
my parents became American
each instance symbolizing a different
version of being American
first is when they decided to stay
and next is the photo of my parents beaming
by a judge with citizenship in their hand
also the photo of my mother and father
in the '60s looking like an American
perhaps foreign only in tongue
the Statue of Liberty behind them
or the first time they're registered
as American by having an American
job   though I was born in America
I wasn't born American
I know it's hard to understand
but it's also not hard I became American
when I memorized the national anthem
or when I had sex with a white boy
or when I thought my first
racist thought or when I decided
I wanted to always live in a place like US
which is how America becomes
an event that happens only for the lucky
so the question *where are you from* means I was born
foreign in America but not their America
I mean the chain of land called America connected
by chains of mountains where minute threads of
the first people who lived that America live in me
when there was the earth giving only over
what she wanted that was before she became American

Icarus Turns Fifty

Crudité and crackers. That's how my own myth starts.
I'm slicing cucumbers when the phone rings with that ominous tone
of a call you are not expecting. *It's happened,* I think. *He's gone and I wasn't there.*

And then comes his voice, alive and unbothered, same as it was,
maybe a tiny bit more gravelly, "Behta?"—and haven't I imagined this moment
a hundred and eight times before, once for each turn in that Minoan maze,
once for each feather individually affixed to my back.

Sometimes I am silent and wait for him to speak, sometimes I hang up,
sometimes I am angry, sometimes I start crying, but in none of them do I do
what I do now, which is respond—conversationally,
as if it hasn't been decades since the labyrinth—"Dad."

Oh, a lifetime since I entered the blue deep, since choking to the surface,
treading water and scanning the thudding horizon for whatever rescue
by bird or boat I thought would come that did not come.

Perhaps it is not surprising that I grew up ordinary, the son of a great genius,
a once-rash once-lad who dared everything to feel fire, to be exceptional,
to reach the sun, to see what fish flickered beneath the dark surface.

He begins in the middle of a sentence, like he always did, talking about the virus
and grocery delivery and what's happening with my cousin's youngest son
who has decided to drop out of college and become a DJ and just like that I feel

the vibration of his voice banishing the old story denying all my anger and sadness
of the decades since I somehow swam through the night to distant rocks,
weeping through my salt-raw throat. And so what is there to say?
I ask him what he shopped for,

and he says they don't have Weetabix and he drinks almond milk now
and the life where I flew away from him and he let me go just winks out
and a new life starts unraveling in its place.

For us there's no epic end, no begging the king of the underworld
to return the lost son, no father casting himself grief-stricken into the sea.
For a moment, I think: he always did invent the most exquisite prisons.

Then I think: or is this what we can bear, is this the price we are willing to pay.
He asks are the cucumbers organic, and did I know they have vegan cheese now.
and did I get those delicious rice crackers or plain saltines.

Kazim Ali

Yield

Why did you not answer when I sent the shrikes to strike
the pane of the sky, what did you hear
when I called out in the night?

I have another life now. We dug up the lawn
and cut back the roses to their roots,
planted instead fava beans, chard, a fig tree, three papayas.

These are things that would never grow in the northern shores:

the great Mexican sunflowers whose seeds the parrots eat,
all the family photographs in which I do not appear,
the one part of my name no one else can pronounce.

It is a kind of hell not knowing whether or not you heard me.
Did you hear me?

The planet continues its spin but I am impaled
on a thorn of silence.

In the city on the mesa between mountain and ocean
we spent days cutting back the lantana so the monarchs
no longer come. In their place we planted avocado trees,
a pomegranate, parsley, and corn.

What could god have said to you that I did not?

We do not break the soil but build on top.
We do not separate the crops but scatter the seeds.
We feed ourselves in every season.

Marco takes bags of beans to every neighbor as a gift
Only one gruffly refuses, saying, "We don't want any of that."
In the night the shrikes come to say what you could not.

In all the years of voiceless song, what have you heard?
On my own and far from my source I had to make a home.
We scattered the seeds. We made a home.

Amor Fati

We wrestled in
the basement, drunk,

my head pressed
hard into the coarse,

blue rug, windows dark.
Upstairs,

my mother stood
at the stove. *Soon,*

my body seemed
to say, turning

under you. It was
1986: the fire

at Dupont Plaza, the
Human

Immunodeficiency
Virus, the

Challenger falling in
pieces over

the Atlantic. You
pinned me

there, bent
so close, I thought

we might
kiss, your shirt

stretched by
my long pull,

and I held on
with both fists.

Passing

Our heads full of someone
else's story, we
empty the theater

without words, and shuffling from
one dark to another, wander home,
the plaza dead, the bar

closed, someone crying in
the street. For what? To whom?
No one
knows. The doors

locked, we lie
in bed and dream
a language of
our own.

francine j. harris

A woman looks at her breasts in the mirror the way

her father would have looked at his chest.
Looking for where the rib, if he were
an evening, then weather would stretch
and light, each eclipse ragged

against night rose, every thump would stereo
stereo. He would touch her
breast the way she would touch
his chest. leaf to pond.

How to Take Down an Altar

First, remove your Mary. Take the chains from her neck.
Then smack out the candles with a pillow. Stack the books

    under Paul in boxes. Lift up
    the snakes. Uncover the faces. Take

        the incense dust in both hands and cross Barbara.
        Unhinge Jesus carefully, at each panel. Move

            the Angels by their buttocks, not their wings.
            Unplug Magdalene. Take away the black gauze

                from the face of Judas. Pull the river foam
                below the roses, lay it under both Moses.

                    Wrap Adam and Eve
                    in light citrus and borax. Make a clay paste

                        to preserve the face of God. Bury the
                        cigarettes. the apple peels. the meat.

Randall Mann

Order

For once, he was just my father.
We drove to the Computing Center
in a Monte Carlo Landau
not technically ours. Lexington,

1977. That fall. The color
had settled, too, undone
orange-brown and dull yellow,
crimson. And it was something,

yet not, the pile of leaves
just a pile of leaves. Sorry to think
what thinking has done to landscape:
he loved punched cards,

program decks and subroutines,
assembly languages
and keypunch machines.
Even my father looked small

next to a mainframe.
The sound of order;
the space between us.
We almost laughed, but not for years—

we almost laughed. But not. For years,
the space between us,
the sound of order
next to a mainframe.

Even my father looked small.
And keypunch machines,
assembly languages,
program decks and subroutines.

He loved punched cards,
what thinking has done to landscape—
just a pile of leaves. Sorry to think,
yet not, the pile of leaves

crimson. And it was. Something
orange-brown and dull yellow
had settled, too, undone
1977, that fall, the color

not technically ours, Lexington
in a Monte Carlo Landau.
We drove to the Computing Center.
For once he was just, my father.

Young Republican

September, 1984.
The heat was like a ray-gun.
The Communists had much to fear:
his name was Ronald Reagan—

and so was mine in middle school,
throughout the mock debate.
The recreation hall was full
of democratic hate.

I ended all my thoughts with *well*,
declared my love for Nancy.
My stifling suit was poly-wool.
I sounded like a pansy.

But teachers didn't seem to care
that Ronald Reagan looked
a little fey, and had some flair.
I wanted to be liked,

the boy who mowed the neighbors' yards,
the new kid in Ocala—
while Mondale read his index cards,
I sipped a Coca Cola

that I had spiked with Mother's gin,
and frowned, and shook my head.
Oh Walter, there you go again,
I smiled and vainly said.

I reenacted getting shot.
I threw benign grenades.
I covered up what I forgot.
I never mentioned AIDS.

Magdalena Zurawski

Of Liberation

You arrive in a sentence
where you would like
to stay, but you are told

to move on to another,
so you do and wish only
this time to keep to imaginary

places. You are not
given Zanzibar or Timbuktu
but Paducah where two

soldiers compare figures on
a motel balcony. You
note the exits and a sign

announcing no free breakfast.
One says, "You look good, man,"
to the other, who nods. Though

you had always understood
figures differently, you
respect their loyalty

to a cause impossible
to understand. "I've been
through two surgeries and

still smell as fresh as
a piano," the admired one
says. The moon is quartered,

and the air is mild. You
sleep in a rented bed
overlooking asphalt. Through

the vents your German
professor repeats, "Ich komme
aus Dodge. Woher kommst Du?"

over and over until your
True Being separates
from a cough that will not

go away. The professor in
the morning seeks out your eye
as he slips out the door,

"To be in a sentence,"
he asserts, "is by
nature to be passing through."

My Life in Politics

Incapable of limiting themselves to petty
offenses, my hands broke into my chest and choked
every slumbering deity.
        After that I no longer cared
to argue about the nature of the flesh. Whether powered by vitalist or
mechanical forces, the spirits had in either case evaporated
as easily as life from the nostrils of a drowned man.

        Oddly, I did begin to care about numbers, but only in exchangeable forms.
"Bread," I heard a man say once
        and it made me a depressive materialist, not
unlike a Franciscan without a dove. I collected frozen peas, greeting each one
like a lost friend, then dispersing them in green streams to the hungry mouths
in the surrounding counties.

        At home I have an old painting to comfort me, a fine example
of Impressionism from the Eastern bloc circa 1981. In the subtle oranges
singeing the trees one sees the foreshadowing of martial law.

        As a child I sat in my Western living room and watched
        the Molotov cocktails fly behind the Iron Drape. Back then no one thought
to explain to me how walls against the flight of capital might end in flames,
how on TV I was witnessing soldiers clip the wings of the very same paper birds
                          that here flew all around me.

Eduardo C. Corral

In Colorado My Father Scoured and Stacked Dishes

in a Tex-Mex restaurant. His co-workers,
unable to utter his name, renamed him Jalapeño.

If I ask for a goldfish, he spits a glob of phlegm
into a jar of water. The silver letters

on his black belt spell *Sangrón*. Once, borracho,
at dinner, he said: Jesus wasn't a snowman.

Arriba Durango. Arriba Orizaba. Packed
into a car trunk, he was smuggled into the States.

Frijolero. Greaser. In Tucson he branded
cattle. He slept in a stable. The horse blankets

oddly fragrant: wood smoke, lilac. He's an illegal.
I'm an Illegal-American. Once, in a grove

of saguaro, at dusk, I slept next to him. I woke
with his thumb in my mouth. ¿No qué no

tronabas pistolita? He learned English
by listening to the radio. The first four words

he memorized: In God We Trust. The fifth:
Percolate. Again and again I borrow his clothes.

He calls me Scarecrow. In Oregon he picked apples.
Braeburn. Jonagold. Cameo. Nightly,

to entertain his cuates, around a campfire,
he strummed a guitarra, sang corridos. Arriba

Durango. Arriba Orizaba. Packed into
a car trunk, he was smuggled into the States.

Greaser. Beaner. Once, borracho, at breakfast,
he said: The heart can only be broken

once, like a window. ¡No mames! His favorite
belt buckle: an águila perched on a nopal.

If he laughs out loud, his hands tremble.
Bugs Bunny wants to deport him. César Chávez

wants to deport him. When I walk through
the desert, I wear his shirt. The gaze of the moon

stitches the buttons of his shirt to my skin.
The snake hisses. The snake is torn.

To Francisco X. Alarcón

(1954–2016)

You made tomatoes laugh
& warned me
some words die in cages.

I met you first in the desert.

You burned sage, greeted
each of the four directions
with plumed syllables.

The ritual embarrassed me—
your stout body, your
mischievous smile did not.

You were familial.

The first poem I wrote
that sounded like me
echoed your work.

Copal, popote, tocayo, cacahuate:
you taught me Spanish
is a colonial tongue.

Some Mesoamerican elders
believed there's a fifth direction.

Not the sky or the ground
but the person right next to you.

I'm turning to face you, maestro.
I'm greeting you.
Tahui.

Eduardo C. Corral

Brian Blanchfield

Salutatorian

Poppy number two is just now molting—
or, what should I call it, a debut? If you
ever took apart a tennis ball, that; plus
the cram of a prom dress inside.
The gender secret, flowering, inversion
version. Last year I picked out and saved
like holy prepuces the split green shells
quartered and shorn and fallen into the bush,
but their shrivel was a disappointment. I'd been
as solemn as a sacrament, retrieving. The breeze
seems to encourage the shirk, and the sun
helps the thick seams to loosen, I think. Not
to record, poetry; to elapse the time it takes. Now
the complex pucker, more open persimmon,
less bunched umber, and the shell like an accent hat
Lucy Ricardo might have windowshopped
in Murray Hill. Then, now, a boy, all of fifteen,
bikes uphill behind me, singing freely
in the voice, half horn, that boys his age
produce and often, if gay, retain. I can tell
it's an anthem, his song, collaborating
with the pump of his pedalwork, along
the easy grade, and to him I'm Idaho
passing through it. I catch "like home to me"
and, belted, "the freeway that never ends,"
showtune big. Back to the blossom,
fist-sized now, or heart-, as they tell you still
in school, for a touchstone. Its predecessor
by a couple days, perhaps in sympathy,
seems to freshen, having been spread
to bright wet pages by the overnight rain,
exposing the inky matrix, blot and pad,
which for now to succeed is to conceal.
A miracle google doesn't know his song.

Learning

These tall—taller than me if today I sit
among them—chandelier weeds, all filament
invisible up from the forest floor more
than a yard away I thought yesterday were
waiting for their moment in the season to unsheathe
whatever torches they would at the far, upward
tips of their muted spray; but coming out
again in the afternoon the wait had been, I saw,
for their moment in the day, to open asters,
perfect sunny fives haphazard in the air,
map pins on a dream-warm itinerary
and every outpost a starry capital.
Every night another year in our prime and
every year a span primeval underground
where the odyssey yet is a closed calendar.

Dear AI, show me a calendar in
a chandler's workshop, show me his
apprentice when he believes himself
alone, show me what happens upon him,
who he feels himself become when through
the cell window the sun through a canopy
warms his brow, cheek, neck, and clavicle.
Show me at his early mouth a flare
if he feels it awakening, plump
and firm and sensitive, seeking, and the tallow,
too, responsive in its redolence
in its vessel, warm bellied and daylit.
Is it a low country, is it renaissance, and
who is the smith or athena of this?

Brian Blanchfield

some said you were the spitting image of evil

after Carrie Mae Weems

you became drum became washboard became
hum became tincan became numb became
cowbell became screendoor became dirtfloor became
skillet became clothesline became dumb became
plow became yardbird became heifer & bitch became
wagon became hitch became bible became barbwire became
strum became headrag became drum became
biscuit became pitchfork became hum became
slopjar became shit became northstar became
pitstop became boxspring became mule became
numb became shotgun became sunflower became
battleaxe became dumb became whisper became

drum—

the distance between what we have and what we want

after Tavares Strachan

chicken anguish   chickenhead language   lost in
translation: Ebonics   Spanglish   pig latin
juke joint conjugation   *what it do*   *what it be*
what it was   lackluster   fuzzbuster   busted
stereotype hype: teeth vs beef   tooth vs
truth   *all that glitters*   something like sequins
weekend heathens   with ashy knees drawn to Jesus
praise be   to the lords of underground
that raised me   in the indigo weed haze
in my negrodian naivete   the white gaze
never phased me   but skittish with skittles
i skedaddle   straddle life & breath   battle
death rays aiming to amaze me   immortal
nothing & errythang twirl: the do or die portal

Gabrielle Calvocoressi

Shave

Like the buck I am I turn my head
side to side. I hear the leaves
rustle. I shake my head a little
and birds reel 'round the forest.
I am no branch. My head turns
to the side. I see out my side
eye. The deep pool of the eye
sees itself pool in the mirror.
I oil myself 'til I am all a lather.
My chest heaves out
so my full heart can abandon
the ribs' stockade. Where
the bullet would go if the hunter
were a good shot: that's
where I place the razor.
I make my skin taut. I pull
my own neck back and to
the side. I come for myself.
Yes, I was a lady once but now
I take the blade and move it
slowly past the jugular, up
the ridge of my chin where
the short hairs glisten. I was
once ashamed. It was a thing
I did in private. My own self
my quarry. No more.
Look how the doe comes 'round
and also the doves and also
the wolf who lets me pass.
The fox offers me the squirrel's
hide to buff myself to shining.
There is no such thing except
the smoothness of my face.

Who Holds the Stag's Head Gets to Speak

Dear God who lives inside the stag's head
even after the stag's shot and lies slumped and abashed
on the forest floor. Protect him.

Even after he's been heaved onto the car's dark roof.
Forest Green. Or Pacific Blue. Nowhere he can see.
His body stiffens like a trellis above the driver.
Help him. Hold him in your sight.

I know the age of prayer is over. I read it on my newsfeed.
Someone said someone said someone said, *Faith is a weapon
of the Man.*

When they take him down in the darkness
he looks like any body. Could you rest the muscle of your breath
against his neck so he won't sag? So the man thinks he's alive
and quakes in the awful company of the risen.

You are the Blue Lord I prayed for when I was hunted.
You came to me through the branches. I could hear you
in the upper room where I had hidden in the cupboard.

The moment the blade goes to gut him please make of his entrails
a phalanx of butterflies. And of his lungs a great bear
charging. My Lord. When I was the cowered beast
you turned me clear as water so the Hunter could not find me.

I beseech you. Abide.

Gabrielle Calvocoressi

Miguel Murphy

Status

Because the storms, white emissions, emissaries
of spring come spilling

winter too—
He looked

into my face
as if leaning into a mirror

he could not
drink. Please—

Your bone structure is superb.
Your fate is haute couture.

As if pleasure had a counterfeit.

As if there were a way to protect yourself
against a vast night slicked inside another

human body. Seed,
tearful silence,

thirst. His face darkening
the gulf in him,

like the truth—
the blood test.

Green moon, cupped shadow.
Skin, my bright cloak.

When he told me, he didn't
know, what could he say—

That wet, ugly glean. His face,
shining like a thirst,

shining in the desert
of contemporary men, like me.

Younger, healthier and eager.

The Sunlight

You wouldn't know it could feel so redundant—
the wolfish starlings plunder the grass
and nothing burns. Big Sur. We came here to rest.
The coast, a color. The thought of nothing,
the blue middle of my life—
                          A cliff side and a footpath
down to the small beach. And fire, there
a cold wind. Long waves the whole year—restless,
leafy and metallic,
                     the brightness of ash. The sunlight
like something from Tarkovsky, one pointless, small ambition
in which passion turns into a terrifying tenderness. Deep
cargo in the hull; heartache. And somehow you knew
you should light the match, like a person condemned
to whom the starlight is
another brief monument to what
                          is fallible. Your life,
little fireling, little warlike starling, flickering indignantly, all
erotic umbrage. Broken wing in my hand. Pathological, shy
flame, I will care for you. Little shape of my fate, my
certain failure. What
                     is desire, if not
this burden. Dearth and glut
cupped in your hands: wild, deadheaded, and blue.

Aaron Smith

Pray the Gay Away

I was a kid and a guy beside me at church
    had an erection. I didn't know

what it was, but it pulsed like a tiny heart
    under his zipper. The preacher

prayed: *Let the holy spirit move through this place,*
    and I thought it was.

When I told my mother I was gay,
    she asked my grandfather to cast out

Satan in the green-carpet living room
    with the orange floral chair.

My grandfather laughed when she told him—
    You know you like girls.

When he put his hand on my head,
    I closed my eyes and saw my father's

dead animals on the wall. Dad's dad
    was in hell because he killed himself,

so was David, the neighbor, who shot off
    his face the day I stayed home from school

with a fever—gunshot across the hill,
    the stay-at-home moms called each other

all afternoon. Mom said God could heal
    my *dirty thoughts* like he did for her

after her hysterectomy. *Say over and over:*
    I rebuke these thoughts in the name of Jesus.

The World of Men

I'm a therapist's wet dream, I say, and he writes
in his notebook, probably, that I'm using humor,
again, to cope. He keeps going back to the doctor
I mentioned, a few sessions ago, who gave me
a prostate exam when I was eighteen. How he made
me strip off all my clothes, saying, *good job*, throwing each
piece on the chair across the room, my underwear
left roped around my ankles. I thought you had to stay
completely undressed while they checked everything.
He lay me down, knees to my chest, went inside, said,
everything feels fine, but it didn't, the crinkled paper wet
from the sweat of my cheek. Still I want to say

maybe that was just his way, that most guys wouldn't
mind being totally naked when he got on his knees,
kneaded between my legs: only his labored breathing
in the empty, white quiet. How many things
happen to us while we don't know they're happening?

Once in a dream I saw myself with a monster
in a white coat eating away at me, while I stood quietly,
not feeling anything. Why didn't I say something?
I've told the story to friends, and they say it's weird,
but was it wrong, does it exist in that confused space
that silences? When I told Mom what happened,
she said, *he was probably just crude*. I think of the ways
her body must have been used, too, without her
understanding. I wondered if it was just the world of men,
my whole life, I'd never figured out how to belong to?

So it made sense when the first man I went to bed with
made me believe I was *silly* for not wanting to do
what he wanted, *just relax, we'll take it slow*. The *no* deep
in my throat as his lotioned finger pushed in, how

I already needed to please. His face changed into
something animal, different from who he was at the bar.
The same ravenous thirst I'd dread with every man,
thinking it might be different if I could just find
the right one, someone who actually liked me.

The one who stood on the bed and came on my face
without asking. The one who left me bruised, then stood
in the door, said, *there might be something wrong with you.*
The one who got on top of me: *you don't look
like your pictures, but I guess you'll do*, and I did,
each time, though I never wanted to, just wanted it
to be over, but for years I tried. What else could I do?
What if this was what love looked like?

Abandoned Palinode for the Twenty Suitors of June

(18th & Sanchez)

It wasn't that the sidewalk offered
admonishment : *Stop thinking about sex.*
It wasn't that kind of neighborhood.
It wasn't the right time of year. Late
spring rode low on the hips, season

long as the inch between his t-shirt
and jeans, long as a city block :
the whole street lived there whenever
he walked by. It wasn't that his room
was small and faced traffic, that in his city

there were five useful verbs : *un-*
button, unbuckle, kneel, open, come.
You were learning to read your body
the way he did : a possible series of
entrances, a fathoming of how deep

the material. What it means to be
entered by a man : an image is the stop
between uncertainties. How, his cock
inside you, his face displayed meaning
where before it had hid inscrutable

and where, afterward, his frank gaze
would close again, a camera's aperture.
Perhaps after all that was the real thrill,
the click of capture, your image folded
in on itself. No matter what pleasures,

what promises, your image—not unlike
eucalyptus, ginkgo or bottlebrush, trees
without fruit that lined his street solely
for ornament and shade—was but shape
he'd pause beneath briefly, considering.

And his body, his image, what were they
to you? Alone, you'd remember his upper
lip's deep dip, his clavicles, their dark lunettes
deepening as he leaned above you, bitter
chicory of his beard, the briefs he preferred

to boxers. A series of lessons in how to read
differently, he was tutor to below grammar.
Your language was changing. *Unbuckle* : a bell
rings with its tongue. *Unbutton* : as plush is
to push. *Kneel* : boot cut. *Open* : the moment

before ink touches paper. *Come* : would you
give it back, his image? Walk back past flyers
tucked under wipers, the row of glass a stun
of sun, to meet yourself before meeting him,
afternoon gathering its proffered romance

and ass, the backward glance that said *yes*?
What would you give up to remain as you
were, a visitor at the corner where cautious
and carnal cleaved and the florist's window
disgorged a forest of orchids? You would

leave yourself uncoupled, untouched,
mouthing nouns all flowers—now round,
now sharp—bachelor's buttons, mums,
agapanthus, protea, poppy, in order to
stop among certainties, imagery of pansy

and lavender, but you could never
again give it up, how *to pleasure* changed
language : floribund, its inflections those
a throat loans moaning, "o" the low notes
bowed strings goad : now gorgeous, now

cut-gut gutteral, all adjective : rapt,
rasped, you went down on his language,
didn't you, wet to the root each uttered
word of the twenty suitors of June? Viking
beard, shaved balls, recurved cock, rancher's

hands, scald scar, Zippo, whiplash, fifteen
cigarettes, the one without money, without
tears, whose mother called, whose armpits
you promised you'd put right here, four
shots and a hard-on, pool cue, nightstick,

handcuffs and rubber boots, taxi, patio,
barstool, bedroom, you fucked them all—
he didn't mind being plural—and you,
in the center of your life, finally changed,
both within your language and without,

as light tilted, slid summer-wise and cormorants
returned the span of their wings to hang black
over shining buoys, waves' crests wind-snapped
like the slack in flags. Beside the lake
you paused, briefly, considered the shape

his image took in the look of things. *Bird* :
bone enough. *Wave* : ephemeral's shell.
Spindrift : to return to air. *Air* : to lean into
lean, lengthening shadows of after afternoon,
how weirdly the planet slanted toward solstice.

TC Tolbert

Imago Dei

(a ghazal, while looking at Roy McMakin's Two Chests:
One with No Knobs, One with Slightly Oversized Drawers)

This is where the shout of someone else's hands is planted. Inside
    stillness. Inside a small light near what is hidden.
Thinking, always, implies the body can be outgrown. Or at least
    become a light in which to hide.

To remove you from view was initially a relief, Melissa. I wonder if
    every word is a lie by omission. Furniture, I believe,
is still in conversation with the forest. Paper too. I am listening for what
    each word, even whispered, wants to hide.

Trans. Queer. White. Passing. Who you have become outside of your
    old names, Melissa. Missy. Moe. So many shears still inside.
Verbally, physically, sexually abused. As a child. As an I. Here is a self-
    portrait as a hiding, ongoing, underneath the hide.

Now I sleep with a pillow on my chest. Before God, I wear wool, linen,
    nylon, and polyester blends. Also MagiCotton™.
And CyberSkin™. Every body I dream in needs pressure of some kind to
    create breath from outside. May we all hide

a little more air in our lungs. The kind that gives flight to flame. The
    kind that buries fire in the tongue. I love you who cannot be touched.
May the small work of speaking be enough to shake God from her cage.
    To protect us. In plain sight we are. She is hiding.

In the outsized chest. In the chest etched with T. In the chest so flat one
    cannot grasp the light stunning what's inside. I praise
every chest and what a chest could be made of. The makers of chests.
    And those who make this more lovely. Living inside a hide.

What I really want to know is how rough, Melissa,

the leaves below the shredded cup of the Aster's
face need to be before it changes species
from Showy Aster to Willow to Rush—*Aster Radula*
being the name of what I thought I was
seeing—fingers first—reading the neck through
touch—a kindness of soft needles—much like the shot I give
myself once a week now—having increased the gauge exponentially
which has the inverse effect on the amount of skin I am
required to surrender in order to wake up in a body I was
told could not live in this world and be loved—

                                                  small

is not a fair synonym for soft—naming you I
have found another way to send my body back
in time to claim how she wants to be
touched—it's been over three weeks and I still can't
find the face of the bird that threatens music—silence—
whatever you want to call it when a well of metal triangles
is rung underwater and poured from the familiar
little mouth of a ghost—

                               every morning I want
to know without drama really how many things I will kill
today—a question of attention—an experiment of turning
god into my body—learning to live in the could-
mean of pine-broken light—

                             when I hid you,

Melissa, I became every man
who tells a woman she would be more safe
if only she would keep herself inside—a hive
of mercies we were backhanded into—unknowingly
praying we wanted to unlearn how to pray—

                                     I am

almost ashamed I could not name it—how little
pleasure I feel when I touch things only
because I am afraid to be

                    touched—

TC Tolbert

Andrea Gibson

Queer Youth Are Five Times More Likely to Die by Suicide

means:
You lived five times harder than you should have had to
to still have a body when you graduated high school.

means:
Hate worked five times harder
to make your spirit its wishbone.

means:
When your mother asked what was wrong,
you were five times more likely to believe you'd lose
her if you spoke the truth.

means:
You were told five times more often
you'd go to hell when you died.

means:
Burning for eternity seemed five times
more doable than another day in the school lunchroom.

means:
You were five times more inclined
to triple-padlock your diary.

means:
You were five times more likely
to stop writing your story down.

means:
I write my heart out now.

I graffiti billboards with the page of my diary
the bullies used to start the rumors.

I tie that page to the end of a kite string and run
a crooked line through the straightest mile
of the Bible Belt.

That page is a protest sign.
That page is a bandana washing
the tear gas out of my lover's eyes.

Queer youth are five times more likely to die by suicide

means:
I sneak into fascist sleepovers
and sharpie my pronouns onto the faces
of senators who voted to criminalize my kisses
when I was nineteen.

I cut the hate out of my mail
and papier-mâché Christmas ornaments
for queer couple whose parents
do not want to know their grandchildren.

I hack high school curriculums and delete
every test that does not ask what the P
in Marsha P. Johnson stands for.

I walk through graveyards with a chisel
correcting the names of trans kids
whose families said, *No,* when asked,
Can you just let me live?

I pace the suburbs with spray paint, editing
the welcome mats of homophobes until they all

speak the truth: that they personally burned
the roof over the heads of *queer youth*
are five times more likely to die by suicide

means:
There are many days I thirst for my own silence
but walk through the desert screaming instead
because I, like most of my queer friends, don't have a child
—I have millions—from Nebraska to Chechnya,

to the Baptist church where I grew up.
My pride in them is a parade I know
won't keep all of them alive, but I keep cutting
my diary into confetti to throw at their hopes

when they float by scared or furious
or laughing or in love and desperate
for the headline to say: *Queer youth*
are five times more likely to:

offer to walk their younger siblings home from school.
To notice the different accents of sparrows.
To find an eyelash and spend twenty minutes
trying to pick what to wish for.

Five times more likely to:

never outgrow blanket forts.
To know there is a word for the scent in the air
after it rains. To see lifelines look like telephone wires
and call a friend who's having a bad day

Five times more likely to:

adore the last man who walked on the moon
just because he wrote his daughter's initials there.
To know there is no universe in which they would not
be proud of their own children.

Queer youth are five times more likely to:

see you how you dream of seeing yourself.
To write something in your yearbook that will get you
through the next decade. To spot a stranger crying
and ask if there's anything they can do to help.

Five times more likely to:
need us to do the same.

Rachel McKibbens

the sandbox

for Lisa or Laurie

We held each other / in silence / mouth against mouth / blood & thunder scorching the grass / Behind the shed / I played the husband / brutish breadwinner / choking her flesh / in my troubled hands / pulling her head back / to lick / from neck to ear / in frenzied thrill / The kind of love / I learned from movies / & what light swamped the air / as I shoved my bald pelvis into hers / blood ripening into wolf brine / burning a girl-shaped hole in the clover? / Every afternoon I became a god reinventing sky / expert forger of the dry hump / I asked *Who's your daddy?* before that was even a thing / Once the recess bell rang / I released her back / into the quiet unwild / to no-longer-mine / to fat white tubs of minty paste / & songs about Jesus / From across the room / I watched my bride / make eyes / with the real boys / & knew I could kill for her / drill a body down into the earth / boy in the Polaroid / a grisly figurine / The white horse of masculinity bucking wild on the inside / I bit my lip & did as I was told / After school / I wanted / to hold her hand / she always wanted a divorce / When the big kids followed me home / calling me / *lesbo* / *homo* / *wetback* / *faggot* / I held my chin out & challenged to fight them all / every time / & why not? / Might as well / we all knew / I would never / win / anything.

salvage

I have learned to need the body
I spent years trying to rid the world of

have learned to cherish its pale rebel hymn
warped by ghost heat, carried, carried

by all my loyal dead. I have learned
to crawl backward into the wilderness

to ask, to eat, to steep in your gentleness.
Let this be where I permit forgiveness

to know you name, to leave our cruelest years
where & how we need them most—

                    behind & unlit.

Ruben Quesada

Driving Drunk

Vodka causes headlights
to blur into an aurora—a spectral mass
writhing like a veil in the distance,
the way our bodies must have
looked under sheets: bicep
to backbone, shoulder held firmly, legs
passing back and forth—the amplitude
of my body falling into you. I see
the sky bruising past pylons
against the downtown skyline. Clouds
crowd into the rear view mirror in shapes
of pink hearts and blue half-moons
like marshmallow Lucky Charms
cereal. Shadows overtake the horizon;
chinks of starlight bedazzle me.

SLC Punk!

The last time we parted, I looked past you
as snow banked along the curb. Patches of sidewalk
glowing brightly, and a wide hunk of clouds hovered above
like the unfinished background of a painting. In the distance

your unbuttoned smile, your blue jeans stirring an electric storm
with its yellow seams sizzling down your thighs. Last night as we lay
in bed, we talked about one-night stands we'd had. You told me
about the time in Salt Lake City where you spent a night in a sling, high

on heroin, and a line of married men waiting their turn to be inside you.
The smell of the fireplace filling your nose is what you remember most.
Beyond the window, mountains blanched with snow. You slowly fade
behind a sugar maple, branches like scarecrows waving goodbye.

Jericho Brown

As a Human Being

There is the happiness you have
And the happiness you deserve.
They sit apart from each other
The way you and your mother
Sat on opposite ends of the sofa
After an ambulance came to take
Your father away. Some good
Doctor will stitch him up, and
Soon an aunt will arrive to drive
Your mother to the hospital
Where she will settle next to him
Forever, as promised. She holds
The arm of her seat as if she could
Fall, as if it is the only sturdy thing,
And it is, since you've done what
You always wanted, you fought
Your father and won, marred him.
He'll have a scar he can see all
Because of you. And your mother,
The only woman you ever cried for,
Must tend to it as a bride tends
To her vows, forsaking all others
No matter how sore the injury.
No matter how sore the injury
Has left you, you sit understanding
Yourself as a human being finally
Free now that nobody's got to love you.

Duplex

The opposite of rape is understanding
A field of flowers called paintbrushes—

     A field of flowers called paintbrushes,
     Though the spring be less than actual.

Though the spring be less than actual,
Men roam shirtless as if none ever hurt me.

     Men roam that myth. In truth, one hurt me.
     I want to obliterate the flowered field,

To obliterate my need for the field
And raise a building above the grasses,

     A building of prayer against the grasses,
     My body a temple in disrepair.

My body is a temple in disrepair.
The opposite of rape is understanding.

Stand

Peace on this planet
Or guns glowing hot,
We lay there together
As if we were getting
Something done. It
Felt like planting
A garden or planning
A meal for a people
Who still need feeding,
All that touching or
Barely touching, not
Saying much, not adding
Anything. The cushion
Of it, the skin and
Occasional sigh, all
Seemed like work worth
Mastering. I'm sure
Somebody died while
We made love. Some-
Body killed somebody
Black. I thought then
Of holding you
As a political act. I
May as well have
Held myself. We didn't
Stand for one thought,
Didn't do a damn thing,
And though you left
Me, I'm glad we didn't.

Bullet Points

I will not shoot myself
In the head, and I will not shoot myself
In the back, and I will not hang myself
With a trashbag, and if I do,
I promise you, I will not do it
In a police car while handcuffed
Or in the jail cell of a town
I only know the name of
Because I have to drive through it
To get home. Yes, I may be at risk,
But I promise you, I trust the maggots
Who live beneath the floorboards
Of my house to do what they must
To any carcass more than I trust
An officer of the law of the land
To shut my eyes like a man
Of God might, or to cover me with a sheet
So clean my mother could have used it
To tuck me in. When I kill me, I will
Do it the same way most Americans do,
I promise you: cigarette smoke
Or a piece of meat on which I choke
Or so broke I freeze
In one of these winters we keep
Calling worst. I promise if you hear
Of me dead anywhere near
A cop, then that cop killed me. He took
Me from us and left my body, which is,
No matter what we've been taught,
Greater than the settlement
A city can pay a mother to stop crying,
And more beautiful than the new bullet
Fished from the folds of my brain.

James Allen Hall

Early English History

Was too early: 8 a.m. Tuesday/Thursday, Elizabeth Hall.
I slouched half-asleep, first-rowed, demarcated
from the frat boys sitting in back so they could see
up the professor's skirt. In the mead hall after,
they surrounded, let me close if I shared my notes.
I was in love with the black-haired outfielder,
his backwards Braves cap, until he called me fag
for refusing to rate our teacher's underwear.
I didn't know how to fight back. I learned that semester
about the rebel queen Boudica, whose revolt razed
three Roman forts and the emperor's temple.
Tacitus provides motive: her husband dead, kingdom
annexed, Boudica flogged, her daughters raped.
The armies she led tortured its captives
but he doesn't say why. Some pain is negligible;
its survival cancels the wound of its birth.
Most accounts say she poisoned herself,
facing defeat. Cassius Dio gives her longer:
secreted away to the south, living unrecorded
for years with her daughters. The boys in my class
drew stick figures fucking on the wall by my room
after I came out. I woke at night to wash out
the crooked glyphs, the caption proclaiming
"AIDES kills faggs dead." I scrubbed until
what remained was fist-sized, vague and pink,
a map of the possible world. Our final project
was to cook an authentic English banquet,
eaten family-style at the professor's house.
At the appointed time in the year of our lord,
I came with dessert but did not see the moat
she'd installed in her foyer. The strawberry pudding
flew like an arrow, pink spurting everywhere,
especially across the faces of those boys whose names

were lost the moment I joined an insurrection
begun in AD 61 by a dissident queen. In the years
since my disappearance, I have cemented
my escarpments, foddered my canon, sewn up
my flag. I am painting my face, bluing my body
with woad. Warn them. I am coming
to punish my Romans.

Romantic Comedy
Enchanted, 2007

Goddamn the snow that sent me into the theater
for two hours' refuge in projected light. Even if
I only wanted escape, goddamn my wanting.
Goddamn the romantic comedy, a genre pockmarked
by selves who never fulfill themselves. Goddamn
the men like me, holding hands next to me in the dark,
their snippets of growl gilding the film, their delight
at the comic heroine's transformation from cartoon
to flesh. She falls from Technicolor to Times Square,
rising from the underground in her marriage gown.
Goddamn her flawless skin, her eyes rinsed red,
waking in a drainpipe at the beginning of a soured century.
And then, God, after the movie's over and I've been flung
into another city's sprawl, after I've been released
from the fold forlorn, damn the bride emerging
from the Renaissance Hotel across the salted avenue,
a vision in an unsullied dress. Goddamn the fabric
so luminous in the portrait, looming from its frame,
filling us with longing to bite it into shreds. Goddamn,
what's wrong with me? I can't stop thinking about the fairytale
princess, her optimism a perfumed wind in a flagging sail.
As if no one is shipwrecked on the shores of Love
Always Fails Us. The groom is whispering, *Goddamn*
you're wet in the hotel laundry to a bridesmaid
whose white fur wrap is a strip of fallen weather
on the cement floor. Goddamn all beauty made in betrayal.
Goddamn the bride, she wants to live the heroine's life,
all shivering lip and beaded veil, goddamn her
until she is weeping, the cartoon fool. The goddamn concierge
opens the car door for her, bending elegantly
at the waist to palm her dress into the limousine.
He fingers the slight hem. Goddamn him, showing us

what he could do to skin on the belly, skin on the thigh,
my untouched cheek. Goddamn the wind, it isn't the hand
of a lover. Goddamn the wineglass shattering inexplicably
at the best man's toast. The best men, the worst men, the extras
in the movie which brought me to tears—goddamn them
and the gift of my body. Goddamn the land and the air,
the fish and the fowl, the light in the day and the night
in the night. But do not damn the lit cigarette I'm holding
too close to my face. Not it, God. Though it burns acrid
between my fingers, it does not leave me alone to lift
my face up out of the halo of darkness, in the cold of Chicago.

Ana Božičević

Carpe Damn

The screen is raining or
bleeding a bit
of white

The edges of the screen are fuzzy
wuzzy

Am I tired or in love

So calm like everything's forgiven
and
the army goes home forever into

The sunset, the forest,
the rain

And I'm beginning. *Je commence*
the long ascent
out of

The screen—I'm outside!
Omfg. Check it out—

The snow is real

Busted Xmas Card

I'm writing a novel
(I think) in which
the things that in this century
are called bipolar
immigrant lesbian
are actual superpowers
Raise your crazy hand if you've imagined
how in another time
you'd be a witch a shaman! or just
another migrant locked up & labored into fine mist
And it's now about that time
Xtians celebrate
the birth of boy wonder
whose trip they dig but
can't quite follow, all over
they're mounting stars on barbed wire
Wow even I bought something
off amazon
a guy earning $12/hr packed it
another walked in the cold
to deliver
identical plastic gold toy trains
to a family tossed by isms straight up war and the art world
And no one was indicted in the prison murder of
#sayhername
There's still time for a ride
to the mall or endtimesy
orgy between friends
dope or daime
before the ball drops
I don't pretend
to understand what goes on
around me

that's my superpower
I don't mind
your gaze from a distance
Who wants to hold the hand anyway
of a damaged refugee liar
Who struggles with you
a great spotted beast in inverted dioramas
where there's such a thing
as the death of the market
and difference and love
are key
They're fucking key

Ana Božičević

Hysteroscopy

After the ultrasound probe sent to search
    for the cause of this raft of blood, ceaseless
    weeks of red on my thighs, the doctor sighs,
lists the fibroids, the thickened walls, the growths
    that *may or may not be worth worrying*
    about. His catalog ends with two words—
unremarkable ovaries—that call
    forth all my unhatched plans. The diagram
    on the wall saws me in half, vertical
axis, organ draped over the bladder
    as if in slumber. This pastel portrait,
    all pallid pink viscera and muted
gold skin, is a sunset that invites me
    in, informs me this place in which all lives
    are made is scarcely the length of my *fuck*
you finger, barely the width of my wrist.
    Uninhabited, the whole shebang—from
    fundus to cervix—is small as my heart,
my fist. The doctor escorts me back to
    this room, this next process in which, to view
    its lining more clearly, he fills my cave
with saline, *like a water balloon.* How
    calm I remain on the table, how still
    for the scope that enters my not-a-womb.
He asks me to rate my pain on a scale
    on which I place a heavy thumb, tip it
    low as a dull headache, as if I'm too
tough for suffering, too butch for distress.
    I hold my breath despite his reminders
    to *relax.* I refuse the stronger meds,
the knockout gas. I want to be awake
    for this moment when I become a home
    to liquid and light, when I am aglow.

In those wilds beyond my parted legs, no
      matter what the doctor finds, a lantern
      now shines, limns the night inside me with stars.
Whatever haunts this dark, may it step forth
      into this circle of fire, lured by warmth,
      may it come forward from the murk, its stark
silhouette against this blaze. At long last
      I will know its name, call it close enough
      to glimpse its tender face amidst the flames.

Jennifer Perrine

Breasts

I can't quit looking when, on the jam-packed train, a woman slips her
tank aside, lifts a nipple to her infant's lips. So casual, like the new mother
at work who leans against a restroom stall, making small talk while the
machine affixed to her chest whirrs away. I want to avert my gaze

but I too know how to objectify, despite my best feminist attempts to
undo what magazines and videos—all those cleavage shots—have taught
me. Once, in lieu of a women's studies exam, I sat with college classmates
to take topless teatime on the quad. I clutched my mug

just so, upholding my activist path. I did my utmost not to gawk, to brush
off taunts, to act natural, but I was not born this way, sporting this klutzy
flapping albatross, swaying lumps that bump and squish against bartops,
that hurt if I so much as jog. At six I first saw through

my older sister the body time would equip me with, how the smooth,
un-broken country over my ribs would round to hills, to dunes shifting
with the wind. I implored every god who might listen to rescue me from
destiny, to exorcize these unruly imps of flesh. Some divinity enjoyed

a laugh at that, delivered an abundance I cannot flatten with any manner
of contraption, except for a binder tight enough to muzzle my breath.
Maybe another deity put in my path each partner who, with one liquid
flick, could conjure a thrill of wonder from what I'd tried to

hide. Surely a higher power placed me among a sea of queens who, before
a pride parade, peeled off my bra, bedazzled my bare skin, whooped as
I shook my jewel-clad moneymakers, my rack, my jugs, my cans, all my
mama gave me, sexy sacks of dense, unused milk glands

that I haul into the doctor each year to be checked for error in the code,
for fatal defect. Now, in the bath, I elect not removal but reacquaintance,
marvel at your vexing heft bent by a hazy plane of water into the optic
trick through which you break our jail, finally float free from me.

Jan-Henry Gray

I-797-C Notice of Action

REQUEST FOR APPLICANT TO APPEAR FOR INITIAL INTERVIEW

APPLICATION NUMBER MSC XXXXXXX058

A# A XXX XXX 961

Notice Date: July 24, 2014

Priority Date: July 24, 2014

Date of Arrival: February 20, 1984

hereby notified to appear
  how often do you have sex
to adjust status
  what color is his toothbrush
his birth certificate
  what side of the bed does he sleep on
resident alien
  how much does he make
your husband must come with you
  what's his mother's name
we may videotape you
  where did you buy your rings
bring an interpreter
  what are his siblings' spouses' names
in a sealed envelope bring
  what's his father's name
failure to appear
  what's *his* father's name
please appear, as scheduled below

  do you love him
supporting evidence
  why do you love him
Tuesday, March 17, 2015, 8:00 a.m. USCIS, Chicago, IL

don't mention citizenship
talk about love, how you got married for love

The Dream Act

There is A GARAGE underneath THE HOUSE.

THE HOUSE has an address.

THE GARAGE does not.

There is A DOOR cut into the garage door.

This is the entrance for THE FAMILY.

THE GARAGE is underneath THE HOUSE.

One night, THE FATHER meets another father who owns THE HOUSE.

They talk about the place downstairs, THE GARAGE underneath THE HOUSE.

THE FAMILY moves into THE GARAGE.

THE FAMILY lives there for THE YEAR.

THE GARAGE is underneath THE HOUSE.

THE FATHER brings home A TREE.

THE FAMILY calls it A CHRISTMAS TREE.

THE TREE is propped on a table in THE GARAGE.

There is no address but there is a telephone line in THE GARAGE.

THE MOTHER is on the phone with her mother.

THE MOTHER is describing THE HOUSE.

THE GARAGE is underneath THE HOUSE.

THE CHILDREN decorate THE TREE with ornaments made of paper.

Natalie Diaz

Why I Hate Raisins

> *And is it only the mouth and belly which are*
> *injured by hunger and thirst?*
> —*Mencius*

Love is a pound of sticky raisins
packed tight in black and white
government boxes the day we had no
groceries. I told my mom I was hungry.
She gave me the whole bright box.
USDA stamped like a fist on the side.
I ate them all in ten minutes. Ate
too many too fast. It wasn't long
before those old grapes set like black
clay at the bottom of my belly
making it ache and swell.

I complained, *I hate raisins.*
I just wanted a sandwich like other kids.
Well that's all we've got, my mom sighed.
And what other kids?
Everyone but me, I told her.
She said, *You mean the white kids.*
You want to be a white kid?
Well too bad 'cause you're my kid.
I cried, *At least the white kids get a sandwich.*
At least the white kids don't get the shits.

That's when she slapped me. Left me
holding my mouth and stomach—
devoured by shame.

I still hate raisins,
but not for the crooked commodity lines
we stood in to get them—winding
around and in the tribal gymnasium.
Not for the awkward cardboard boxes
we carried them home in. Not for the shits
or how they distended my belly.
I hate raisins because now I know
my mom was hungry that day, too,
and I ate all the raisins.

American Arithmetic

Native Americans make up less than
1 percent of the population of America.
0.8 percent of 100 percent.

O, mine efficient country.

I do not remember the days before America—
I do not remember the days when we were all here.

Police kill Native Americans more
than any other race. *Race* is a funny word.
Race implies someone will win,
implies, *I have as good a chance of winning as*—

We all know who wins a race that isn't a race.

Native Americans make up 1.9 percent of all
police killings, higher per capita than any race—

sometimes *race* means *run.*

I'm not good at math—can you blame me?
I've had an American education.

We are Americans, and we are less than 1 percent
of Americans. We do a better job of dying
by police than we do existing.

When we are dying, who should we call?
The police? Or our senator?
Please, someone, call my mother.

At the National Museum of the American Indian,
68 percent of the collection is from the United States.
I am doing my best to not become a museum
of myself. I am doing my best to breathe in and out.

I am begging: *Let me be lonely but not invisible.*

But in an American room of one hundred people,
I am Native American—less than one, less than
whole—I am less than myself. Only a fraction
of a body, let's say, *I am only a hand—*

and when I slip it beneath the shirt of my lover
I disappear completely.

How the Milky Way Was Made

My river was once unseparated. Was Colorado. Red-
fast flood. Able to take

        anything it could wet—in a wild rush—

            all the way to Mexico.

Now it is shattered by fifteen dams
over one thousand four hundred and fifty miles,

pipes and pumps filling
swimming pools and sprinklers

    in Los Angeles and Las Vegas.

To save our fish, we lifted them from our skeletoned river beds,
loosed them in our heavens, set them aster—

      'Achii 'ahan, Mojave salmon,

           Colorado pike minnow—

Up there they glide, gilled with stars.
You see them now—

      god-large, gold-green sides,

           lunar-white belly and breast—

making their great speeded way across the darkest hours,
rippling the sapphired sky-water into a galaxy road.

The blurred wake they drag as they make their path
through the night sky is called

        'Achii 'ahan nyuunye—

                our words for *Milky Way*.

Coyote too is up there, crouched in the moon
after his failed attempt to leap it, fishing net wet

        and empty slung over his back—

                a prisoner blue and dreaming

of unzipping the salmon's silked skins with his teeth.
O, the weakness of any mouth

        as it gives itself away to the universe

                of a sweet-milk body.

As my own mouth is dreamed to thirst
the long desire-ways, the hundred thousand light-year roads

        of your wrists and thighs.

Tommye Blount

André Leon Talley's Caftan

No matter what the haute monde have deemed me,
I know that I'm still a boll of cotton

that remembers what existed before: whiteness,
barbed and prickly, so angry it broke skin

after it broke families apart—I go back to that time
before the ateliers and their banditry of swift hands,

back to where I was raised from the dirt
and the fields, darling, I've never forgotten

from whence I've come, to the flesh my husk
once opened, I return now to husk in luxury.

Diva Worship

Teena Marie

In the slick groove
she slips a funky toe,

then puts her whole
ole nasty foot in it;

gives us her soul
then becomes our sole

ivory goddess, our rent party
patron, our blues-eyed lady

in the blue light; she enters
our houses, we make room for her,

move the furniture to the wall,
roll back the rug,

get down when she sings
"Everybody get up."

*

Esperanza Spalding

In Bantu knots, Ebony
Arachne, she dares challenge the gods

of jazz; all hands getting busy
with a theory of strings;

cradling catgut with a witch's will;
resting at her loom,

Penelope singing with her eyes closed,
hauling around that big old vessel's weight.

*

Vanessa Williams

A star darkening their white pageantry,
how high you resigned yourself,
a colored gone with the wind of stardom,
a high-yellow Tituba to burn,
a witch playing around
in Sondheim's woods, top billing
in the Playbill, a sure bet on Billboard,
a farce gone fierce on BET, disrobed diva
dethroned to save their white faces,
in the boob tube, there she is,
Missed Black America.

*

Phyllis Hyman

"Whoa oh I can't stand this living all alone,"
I always want to say in a poem,
but that's your line—the tether

we thought kept you on this side
of the bridge. The note, what are we

to do with the note you left? I heard it
on the radio. Your voice coming out
of our mouths as if we could

take some of that sadness from you,
try it on like shoulder pads, a fly hat,

as if that would save you now. How
are we supposed to reach you now?
We don't have the range.

Shelley Wong

For the Living in the New World

There are so many ways to explore a forest—
over clover clusters, past skunk cabbages

to a field where we listen for a ghost
of song. The hypergreen periphery

is the opposite of Los Angeles on fire.
Any tree can become a ladder. These trees have

too many branches, but it is not my place
to revise them. I may be happiest

improvising the language a body can make
on a dancefloor. We are just learning

how female birds sing in the tropics.
Spring insists we can build the world

around us again. How has love brought you
here? My head is heavy from the crown.

Private Collection

At the San Francisco Museum of Modern Art
the ocean drawn in pencil is no longer
on display. I once thought *I could wreck*
that water. My partner liked a painting

of a blonde woman reading a newspaper,
a sister to a Dutch painting I admired
back in New York, where a woman
contemplates a water pitcher

in cathedral light. We walked gallery to gallery
& no women resembled us. I'm charmed
by certain French words, but forget what they mean
& never properly pronounce them—

mélange, de rigueur, au courant. Sometimes
couples become echoes of one another.
We wore quiet glasses, our hair in low ponytails
like George Washington. She would photograph me

when I looked away from her, as I glanced
at the curves of the Grand Tetons, the raised head
of the Greek caryatid locked in the British Museum,
a winter forest floor

somewhere in Oregon when we were nineteen
& I couldn't meet the camera's gaze,
though I knew she was there & that she
would hold me from a distance.

Rajiv Mohabir

Upon Stumbling Across a Beached Bottlenose Dolphin Carcass at Provincetown

I walked the curl of the Cape
into a cove, the fishhook
of earth and found washed up

on a February shore
the carcass, its gray whitened
with bird shit, eyes

missing, a new blowhole pecked
into its skull. Did it ignore

kin and pod though they
cried out in fall sun,

Come home, Come home
seeking instead a short-lived joy?

I have taken this other
world for my own—

morphed into a haramkhor,
eater of evil: who rips out
pages of the creation story. Once

the sea was a sea
of milk. Once summer
was a sea

of men. In the beginning
there was water
until I drank,

reckless, my beard soaked
and dropping diamonds.
After the beginning, a pause,

the silence
of winter ice,

the silence of night
meeting night.

Pandemic Love Poem

One by one
the yellow jackets
leave their nest,
a hole covered
with decaying leaves
that warm the ground
and an inert queen
they've fed
all autumn. What sleeps
inside will one
day burst into
a wind of wings.
What will wake
a sleeping queen?
Beneath my waist
growing larger,
the sting of nights one
by one, when
I am stranger and
stranger to you.
We sleep in a converted
porch, wooden siding,
the wall that insulates
what's inside it
which is not you,
nor is it me.
The bedclothes stiffen
with cold. Remember
me? One by
one peel the yellow
sheets from our nest. Prick me
with your heat

from sleep. Place
a cardamom pod
under my tongue.
Come, dissolve
with me.

Vanessa Angélica Villarreal

Bestia

little whip   study the map   in the moon take
this pink comb   a lighter   and this limp-spined
wallet   mira   I put this   paper in it: THESE
ARE THE INSTINCTS   YOU WILL NEED   TO CROSS
stay in the light   do not wait   for anyone
except for the   little one   these are the phone
numbers   do not make friends   these are the
safe houses   & the women who   will repair
your shoes   nice men are never nice   when they
are starving   if they ask you   who is waiting
en el otro lado   for you   tell them no one
that every step   is a prayer   for the impossible
pay the coyote   this amount   put the rest asi
in your panties   put it even   where love
cannot cross   but mija   you are loved our
prayers   will protect you   this land   has
always belonged   to you   don't cry   don't be
afraid   don't cry   don't be afraid   don't cry
don't be afraid   no llores   no tengas miedo

Girlbody Gift

first dress as a boy / an earlied eleven / iron papi's khakis a
dickies crease with white t-shirt / gel-comb black slickback
como linda / me and my girls look hard / get caught / papi's
hands crush my neck / *si no te compones / te voy a matar /
aquí no quiero jotas* // first kiss twelved / chauncey saturnine
centaur / trembling to jodeci // first boyfriend tyrone mj
smile / you want to go with me / spiral perm and boyz II
men II / sleep in his rockets jersey / papi's backhand / *no
quiero que andes con los pinches negros* // first against / light-
eyes cedric / dream prince of pines / appears at sleepover /
the moon is a pill in my can / dazed I kneel / dick a dark
poppy / no a muffled petal in my throat / not all my yet / tells
his boys // first white boy / summer night a stolen sapphire
/ justin shooting stars on slide / three am taut orchid drum
/ mami pregnant due to work at seven / searching the milky
fog / caught in her chevy's headlights / get the belt / *slut* to
his boys // bi furcate my head / shave bottom half / rocks pelt
my back on track / get the belt / *faggot dyke freak* / and with
all my new names / I can now fathom my father / his father
/ saying all the things he doesn't want me to be // hospital
roommate nicole / lily-firm breasts on sterile white sheets /
hillary pink vodka mattress / leigh on tina and a yearning of
triangles // seventeen / doctor writes hymen intact // a knot
hot and sharp as woodsalt / on the chord in my starheart

Donika Kelly

Self-Portrait with Door

Compton, California, early 1990s

Do you remember the princess
locked in a tower, a doorless room
because her father feared a grandson
who might kill him? And the god, who slid
into her room as light as rain as gold,
a deluge she bore and later bore him
a son who would kill a king?

Well, this is not that.

A girl awakens in a room, the door
unpainted, with no knob—just a hole
where the knob could be. Eyes closed,
she imagines the lock. She imagines
locking herself inside. She imagines
her father knocking, the lock a rebuke.
Imagines his disappointment at the door,
which cannot yield. Imagines sleeping
through the night. Imagines him still,
standing at the locked door.

This is not that.

I open my eyes. He is standing
at the foot of my bed. He has pushed
the open door, pushed open the room
as a man. Tonight, he will pin me
to a wall in the open room, frottage
between my thighs, and I will bear him.

Another night, he will take me
in the kitchen and I will bear him;
or the laundry room and I will bear him;
or the bedroom he shares with my mother.

I will bear him wherever I am taken
and no one will kill him and he will not die.

from *The Catalogue of Cruelty*

Once, I slapped my sister with the back of my hand.
We were so small, but I wanted to know

how it felt: my hand raised high across
the opposite shoulder, slicing down like a trapeze.

Her face caught my hand. I'd slapped her in our
yellow room with circus animals

on the curtains. I don't remember
how it felt. I was a rough child.

I said *No*. I said *These are my things*.
I was speaking, usually, of my socks:

white, athletic, thin and already gray
on the bottom, never where I left them.

I was speaking of my fists raining down
on my brother's back. My sister's. Socks.

In the fourth grade, in California,
I kicked Charles in the testicles. At that school,

we played sock ball: hit the red playground ball
with the sides of our hands and ran the bases.

I kicked Charles with the top of my foot, caught him
in the hinge of ankle. I wanted to see

what would happen. I didn't believe
anything could hurt like it did on TV.

Charles folded in half at the crease of his waist.
My god, I was a rough child, but I believed

Charles, that my foot turned him to paper.
Later, I kicked my dad the same way,

but he did not crumple. It was summer
in Arkansas. What humidity,

these children, full of water. I hit him
also with the frying pan. I hit him

also with the guitar. We laughed later:
Where had the guitar come from? My dad

was a star collapsing. The first thing
a dying star does is swell—swallows

whatever is near. He tried to take us
into his body, which was the house

the police entered. This is how I knew
he was dying. I'd called the police.

What is your name? He tried to put us through
the walls of the house the police entered,

which was his body. *What is your name?*
Compromised: the integrity of a body

contracting. *What is your name, sir?* He answered:
Cronos. He answered: *I'm hungry.* He answered:

A god long dead. He threw up all his children
right there on the carpet. After all,

we were so small, the children. The thing
about a star collapsing is that it knows

neither that it is a star nor in collapse.
Everything is stardust, everything essential.

What is your name? Everything is resisting
arrest. Its gravity crushes the children

and the cruiser's rear passenger window.
The officer didn't know the star's name.

White dwarf? Black hole? To see: throw the collapsing
star face-first into anything. Face-first

into the back seat. Face-first into the pepper
spray. Face-first onto the precinct lawn.

Did you know you could throw a star? Do you
understand gravity, its weaknesses?

*You are in my house. You should already
know my name.*

DONIKA KELLY

Charif Shanahan

Dirty Glass

By now, we are used to this routine—
the airports, the trains, the long,
deliberately silent farewells.
I wait until the train doors close.
The dirty glass window between us,
I turn to exit the platform. Zürich waits
for you and I ride the escalator out
of Penn Station, past the pretzel carts,
onto the smoky streets ravaged by
the absoluteness of winter. I do not know
if I love you. There is nothing for me here
in this angry, automatic city, and you
promise me love, a home, even money.
I notice no one, walking to the subway
toward another fatherless night
in the Bronx, where I'll sit in silence,
drinking hot tea to scald the place
in my body where the pain roots.

Control

In the Pornhub video two houseless men
Suck each other on a subway bench.
It's late at night, but not late enough
No one is around. The people are
Outraged, call the men disgusting.
New York and humans disgusting
While they continue to record.

I have the space inside my body to feel
The two men, their commitment
To pleasure, absent basic comfort:
The one's face nearly neutral, as though
His friend's mouth and the sting of existence
Canceled each other out. Almost
Like a mannequin. Just there.

        On Hyde Street
Yesterday morning, walking briefly
In no clear direction, I saw a man
On the opposite sidewalk, a motorcycle
Parked at a right angle to his feet.
He put one hand on a handle, the other

On his crotch, and glared above the slow-
Moving traffic at me. The question
In his face, its own answer.
        When I tell you
I don't know what to do with my life,
I mean I don't know how to stay inside it.

Joy, Gary says, *is a feeling of profound gratitude—*
And before I can ask for what—*for having come*

How far I have come. I celebrate with my friend
And think at once: We should be grateful then
For surviving a country that makes of survival

A victory and not a right? We talk about
Our boyfriends, syntax, Nella Larsen's *Passing*.
Gary leans across the couch to touch my chin.
We were lovers once, briefly. I look at him
Look at me. *Try to love yourself, darling.*

He says. *You're going to be here a long time.*

Wound

It has taken me years to begin this poem.
   I have not known from where to speak.

Because I had not been positioned,
   I had not positioned myself to speak.

In this way, it has taken me years
   To begin not only this poem but being

A person at all, which is required
   For speaking, it turns out, which is,

Frankly speaking, the thing I have most
   Wanted, most needed to do,

Not for my ego, not exactly, but
   To clear what had positioned me

In the first place in no place.

      Charif Shanahan

from *Nature Poem*

We are the last animal to arrive in the kingdom—even science will tell
you that.

My father takes me into the hills we cut sage. He tells me to *thank the
plant for its sacrifice, son.* Every time I free a switch of it a burst of
prayer for every leaf.

I'm swoll on knowing this? Sharing the pride of plants

My mother waves at oak trees. A doctor delivers her diagnosis.

When she ascends the mountains to pick acorn, my mother
motherfucking waves at oak trees. Watching her stand there, her
hands behind her back, rocking, grinning
into the face of the bark—

They are talking to each other.

I am nothing like that, I say to my audience.

I say, *I went to Sarah Lawrence College*

I make quinoa n shit

Once on campus I see a York Peppermint Pattie wrapper on the ground,
pick it up, and throw it away. *Yr such a good Indian* says some dick
walking to class. So,

I no longer pick up trash.

I want to be the one who eats the candy
at the Felix Gonzalez-Torres exhibit, not the one splashing his face
with cold water in the bathroom

but we r who we r

like jambalaya.

Let's say I was raised on television and sugar and exhausted parents
working every job that poked its head from the tall grasses of opportunity

who didn't go to college but still read poetry to each other and wrote
songs and made sculptures and read law documents at the beach while I
threw like seaweed on my cousins
but opportunity to what?

My current envy list includes ppl who make decisions, in general.
Envy is a shit tit. I meet a boy and I miss him. Time, a paragon of
confidence, taps me on the shoulder and asks

if I get legit anxiety when someone calls from a number I don't know,
cos it's like—who still calls?

I've always wanted to know, I say, *why they call you Father*

You can't reflect and decide at the same time. If language is a structure
born of the desire to communicate, can I really be blamed when
Money says *anxiety is only real when the face breaks* and I'm chipping
like paint?

I shoot thru yr stupid sky like a stupid sky

You are like the third convertible in a row or like seafoam socks in the
fat far rockaways

I can't look you in the eye and listen
at the same time. Yr not stupid at all, you say things like "the skin of
art," but here with me in the back of this margarita—you must be very,
very stupid

Ppl here wear stupid shirts that button all the way up to the top of the
tower, and inevitably fall

I look too much into the mirror of my worst self
so life feels like always breakin in a pair of new shoes
and my hunch is we'll be naked soon having sex like those handsoaps
that smell like parsley sort of refreshing but chemical Nothing like the
real thing n you wd prolly notice if we fucked with all my clothes on
bc yr of course so hazel
and stupid.

Nothing can fall that wasn't built

except maybe my self-esteem bc I have a hunch that I was born with it
intact but then America came smacked
me across the face said *like it*
n the sick thing is getting smacked across the face makes me so wet rn

and that's prolly why poetry, bc in order to get inside
a poem has to break you
the way the only thing more obvious than your body
is leaving yr shirt on in the pool.

The perigee moon haloes the white comforter in a Beyoncé way.

You shine like a bar of soap in the shadows.

The perigee moon is above both of us, in Portland, in NYC, in San
Diego, in Hong Kong, Abu Dhabi, Guaynabo, Sri Lanka

Knowing the moon is inescapable tonight

and the tuft of yr chest against my shoulder blades—

This is a kind of nature I would write a poem about.

Meg Day

On My Way to Meet Her in Liberty Park Before the First Snow

I walk tilted forward so as to let the violent wind anoint my head
or take it from me. Lord, you give me so little courage:

like a ship aimed seaboard, wavering in the surge, I come to you
listing & hungry for cert, rushing each gust's inhale with the beams

of my legs, lurching in empty airstream toward some chance harbor
invisible behind that solid hill of green slurry. Why, as I tear

toward it, won't you right me? A chalk wharf only lends refuge
with a lighthouse to baptize its mouth—& though this full season

wills all its ochre leaves to fold around me the grandest
of canyons (the wind bending its breath through the harmonica

of pines), no amber is bright enough to project the forecast
as shadow or shade. Is it water that carves the gully to gorge

to valley, or the sheer face of rock that bows, a deep grin,
& rips open at its seam to welcome the flood?

When They Took Her Breasts, She Dreamt of Icarus

When they took my breasts, I dreamt of Icarus
& woke each hour to the blurry hands & heads
of Briareus in a white coat struggling to keep my arms
from flapping & the mercury in its glass.
They had lost me on the table, or so Icarus said,
& in the slow-motion scramble for paddles
or pulse, we flung our bodies, arms widespread,
& flew a flat line to the sun in crimson exodus.
I, too, am the son of a craftsman, I told him later
at my bedside, *a master of time & the pieces that keep it.*
We spit, then, & shook, palms all wax & feather,
two brothers proved failures in such lineages of merit.
That night he slept behind me, our curved spines yawning
& when the sun rose they punctured both lungs to keep me from drowning.

When the pain was too much, they gave me Icarus
& he'd sit beside me while they emptied my drains,
or sing refrains of Fugees covers while doodling airplanes
flying close to the sun. He'd question my sutures,
Are you killing him softly with your song? & fall
to the floor in fits of laughter, my smile brighter
when we knew the cancer'd gone. *You'll be lighter
without all that weight,* he told me one night from the hall
& I lay alone in the dark watching the IV drip,
knowing he meant breasts & not the tumors that took them,
a flat-chested emblem of our future flight in tandem,
a handsome membership to—no, abandon ship.
I never wanted to be less woman. But I was
more monster than man, a leviathan in gauze.

When he fashioned my new breasts, Icarus did not use wax
or feathers, wristwatches or wings. He used caution & hesitation
& the cauterizing of things; he slapped warning labels on my decision,
instructed judgment to form a line at the door. *If you relapse*
it'll be the last time, he continued, miming the surgeon, scalpel in hand.
I've always said hubris was stored in the chest & they stitched in my pride,
one bag for each side. Later, when the drains were replaced & the sutures retied,
he asked if I ever thought about death: *Pearly gates? A big brass band?*
When I die, he said, *I hope I go in autumn; I hope I leave*
with the heat of the sun still burned brown at my nape
& the thick gusts of equinox searing up under my cape;
I hope there is ocean enough for my scattering, & still sea left to grieve—
O, how I'd come to crave the surprise of death instead of its prediction:
let me be amazed by my departure, let it be some unafflicted eviction.

Cody-Rose Clevidence

from *This Household of Earthly Nature*

why not watch a relaxing 2 hour live squid cam from the Monterey
Bay Aquarium?   a YoutTube time-lapse video of Pangea splitting apart
zoom out to me standing in my kitchen dicing summer squash   sautéing its pale
green flesh in bacon-fat and lemon juice   the James Webb Telescope is
taking pictures of the early universe   my dogs are asleep on the couch covered in
stars. permission to be happy   permission to feel alive   permission to not be in
pain   permission to let the dying things die   permission to not think
about dying   permission to let the wine turn to vinegar in the glass
the bread rises somewhere between the yeasts and the singing

the morphology of the molting universe
all the prayers of the whole world, poured into a small cup

pour it out for us

the billions or trillions of yeasts and bacteria and viruses in a single cup
a single breath a bellybutton a glass of rainwater an inch of dirt

a fly stuck in eden's net
a million flies a million webs
the photoreceptors in each fly's eye
like this the world kaleidoscopes outward and inward
folding, unfolding, to calculate a prayer

to calculate the trajectory of each atom in motion
would be to predict the entire future

no, say that there is randomness built into the system
slight perturbations in an unstable equilibrium
as if it were a vast and seamless net flowing into time
as if we were fish returning to the rivers of our birth

hatchlings in the vast and seamless nest, so weave—
we are hard-wiring the universe outside of time
just for this one small moment on earth
a blip here a blip there, blinking once or twice
folding over, maintaining this little
disequilibrium we call a household, a
body, what living is

decay of unstable orbit   caterpillars
are eating holes in the mainframe, fish
are spawning and dying in the rivers, don't worry,
this is how it has always been

this is the efficient flow state of matter between time and time
this is where we will build the nuclear reactor
this is where the asteroid hit

don't worry, it is improbable you will fall through the electromagnetic
net of the atoms of the universe and come out the other side, awake—
unless...? don't worry, the world will hold you.
the world is holding you now.

accept the superconductors, reject the citrus
the price of a shipment of fish, you can grow
vanilla beans in Texas, I order rose harissa on eBay
$52 for a lot of 10 jars & "free shipping" from
the "united kingdom," I order vanilla beans
from Madagascar, I spend all evening sitting
on a bucket with an aluminum beer can
on the ground next to me, connecting different pipe
and hose fittings to a small transfer pump, splitting
the existing water line with a brass barbed coupling,
moving between different pipe threadings, diameters,
affixing the black poly pipe with hose clamps, installing
air vents, splits, shunts, diversions and bypass lines.

it is all a project of planning, of forming the imaginary
system, drawing diagrams, thinking about air pressure,
gravitational pressure, fluid dynamics, what path water
might take inside the unseen, unknowable black-box of
black tubing, laminar versus turbulent flow, of fitting forms
to their available components dumped out of the blue
Lowes bucket onto the dirt ground in front of me, ultimately
to direct the world to my own more human ends
—this finite and particulate world inside the world—an acre
is what a person can plow in a day—in this case to direct the
available water from a distant spring into my catchment tank
so I can water my garden, take showers, do dishes.

the lead or copper pipes of each city singing through their geometric tangle,
happily pumping the water up and up, bless

wait, what—?

ritual motions of each level   the taste of sweetness or putrefaction
binocular vision   fiat currency   copper mines
city-zoning-commission-board   choices
corroded lead   zinc   flagella
how did we get here   how long it took us to get here

O nucleotide: shining rungs on the ladder; up. sugar & acid, up and up
O, twirl, you helix of abacus—round moon to the left over, yellow shell station sign
to the right, beads pressed between thumb and forefinger, seeds or carapace crushed
between teeth, concrete excrescence, our human histone proteins same as yeast, the
exoskeleton of my mind growing outward, gnawing at the hard edges, the
innumerable lineages, the symbiotic flow of time, logging back into the network

first to conceive of, then to obliterate
heretic: of weeping, small stones, hieratic,

an email from my mother, a quarter cup of rain
the Large Hadron Collider moans in the distance
the gulls fall from the cliffs and then glide out over an ocean
today, or one hundred
million years ago?
there is a stillness, and then there is the breaking

there is a stillness, and then there is the breaking.
impossible burgers, "meatless meat," 3d printed eukaryote
of my same soul held in my same hands. there is the heat
and then there is the shadow, there is a certain pressure
in the air, we all share the weight of it, there is a relief
that will come after. I promise. I hope. there is somehow
a net amount of material on this here earth, just always shifting
between forms. "or I may be a simple drop of rain,
but I will remain..." "and now it seems to me the beautiful
uncut hair of graves" "and again and again and again" the rows
of sugar beets stacked in the fields, the smoke rising up,
graffiti on the overpass, how can we hold it all together?

upon closer inspection, the world is not, in fact, falling apart.

palindromic multiverse   shell-company   voiced syllabics sung out loud
one potato   two potato   three potato   four   what was once a root
caloric intake [of our] dominion   what was once a root   gigantic
and us with it   the shining monoculture fields of corn stand
irrigated in the desert   everything besides remains

in the high stone cliff: stone cities of the dead
one overlooking the ocean, one overlooking the river
the ocean necropolis and the river necropolis

we think even the dead might like to look out
of their stacked high stone honeycomb apartments

between the arched columns
from their dark expansive interiors
cut into the side of the mountain,
all together, in the mornings.
like this memory is witness

like this a hole for memory is carved into rock
to hold the data of all the souls

like this memory is the braid that braids the past to the future
memory is the imagination of the past   a time
held out of time   held in the hands of our minds
carried forward   ancestors and ghosts   placed in our altar

memory is a vessel with a million holes
we pour it back and forth between us, sieve to sieve

memory is broken-off fragments of the real
mutating, evolving, growing strange inside us
the mind is an ecosystem of divergent memories
coming together, coming apart, we roll
the universe down the hill together
and one by one we roll it back up

Alex Dimitrov

August

So this is love. When it slows
the rain touches everyone on their way home.
Whatever was promised of pleasure
costs the body more than it has.
Perhaps they were right putting love into books...
to look at the sky without asking a question,
to look at the sea and know you won't drown today.
Despite all our work, even the worst of life
has a place in memory. And the fixed hours
between two and five before evening
are the aimless future with someone
who cannot stay new. August returns us
to a gap in history where our errors
find the invention of a kinder regret.
Almost possible: to believe these days
will change more than us but the past, too.
Which is blue and without end.
A long drive toward a remembered place.
A secret left on a beach. Underwater
where the voices of summer are tones of speech,
requiring less of the mind. The familiar creaks
in the old floorboards. Glasses left out in the storm.
Our handwritten lists with every illegible worry
and yes. The person you think of
despite their cruelty. The sun and its cruelty.
How it's kept its distance and kept us alive.
Not needing to know anything about what we do
with the rest of desire.

New Moon

Wherever you are tonight
and whoever is with you,
small fist the earth is
if one new moon can charm us.
It likely won't change you this once
or resolve your real worry
about romance and death, friendship
and time, the narrow hallways
we'll walk unaccompanied
by anyone we know.
It is not too late for ardor.
It is not yet late enough for less.
What could fill description
like the moon or New York City?
Maybe chance and every river,
how our mothers look in spring.
It's motherless up there. Then quiet.
And our names—the names
we tried so hard to live with—
are no longer ours. They're
just sound. They're mere color.
They have never wanted us less.

Rachel Mennies

How Grandmother Paid Her Passage to New York

One by one her mother sold her silver spoons
and heirloom bracelets, goodbye, porcelain bear,
silk blouses, patent-leather Mary Janes, the scarves
and stud earrings for newly pierced ears, the red wool coat
spotted walking on another tiny body's shoulders
down *Wittenbergplatz*. Goodbye, books bound
in leather, bone china, even the hangers, the goblets
and cabinets; goodbye to the Torah buried in the backyard,

the neighbors, the schoolmates, the mothers dressed so well
at services, the men with businesses who stayed behind
one week, two weeks more. What stylish
objects they became: the coins from fillings
and wedding rings, the soap, the wigs, lamp
after lamp to light a thousand decorated homes.

I Learn of Slaughter

Sunday in the supermarket,
all the Kosher meat's expired. I think
of the chicken pulled from its cage, forced
to hear Hebrew as the rabbi sanctifies it, slits

its throat. Last comfort for a surely Jewish
terror: waiting and waiting for a death
that's coming soon, death that we march from or to
in all our liturgical texts, death that's felled so many

from the photo albums, the dinnertime stories—
don't come for us, not yet. When history
says it's time, when we've worn out
our welcome, grown fat from the farmer's

land, lulled by the sweet sound of praising
God, death will come: the knife
so heavy in our neighbor's hand.

Rapture

Wet pink shock of a sliced-open
peach, pit hard between our teeth,
reached in a liquid, honest hurry.
Peach in the fingers of a certain lover's hand.
Peach juice sliding down the wrist of a man
with assertive hungers. Peach, bringer
of rapture: the climax, but not
the fall. Peach sky rising up and up, free
of consequence. Impossible, but for
our chase of it. Peach in the crisper drawer,
softening. We hear stories of the pastor
and his book, so certain of fire, his biblical
calculus. Peach hot, sugared in an oven.
The mouth of red around the brain-
shaped, dumbstruck stone. Peach the very taste
of sin. Peach that sends the crows circling,
rapture here and gone. Peach God, rapt for carrion,
turning above us in the heavens, waiting for
us, ripening, to satisfy ourselves;
come to him pitted, come to him
finished, made rotten by
your sweet time in his sun.

Boy Found Inside a Wolf

Red is at the end of black. Pitch-black unthreads
and swings garnet

in what I thought was home. I'm climbing
out of my father. His love a wet shine

all over me. He knew I would come
to this: one small fist

punching a hole
to daylight.

Drag

The dress is an oil slick. The dress
ruins everything. In a hotel room
by the water, I put it on when
he says, *I want to watch you take it off.*
Zipping me up, he kisses the mile
markers of my spine. I can't afford
this view. From here, I see a city
that doesn't know it's already
drowning. My neck shivers from
the trail of his tongue. I keep my
eyes on the window, just past
his bald spot. He's short. I can see
the rain that has owned us for weeks
already. The dress will survive us.
The dress will be here when men
come in boats to survey the damage.
He makes me another drink, puts
on some jazz, and the dress begins
to move without me. Slow like some-
thing that knows it cannot be stopped,
the dress seeps. The dress slides
with my body floating inside,
an animal caught in the sludge.
If he wraps his arms around me,
it will be the rest of his life.
I don't even know what I am
in this dress; I just sway with
my arms open and wait.

Alive at the End of the World

I hear the sirens and run
a hand over my silhouette,
surprised not to find bullet
wounds, burns, or history,

but now, ambered under
this streetlight, he pulls me in
for a kiss again and I decide,
briefly, to let the world kill

itself however it chooses: yes,
I hear the sirens and I am their
scream but tonight, I will moan
a future into my man's mouth.

Sam Sax

Treyf

feygele is yiddish for the way i walk into a room.

feygele, the anglicized spelling of angel

fallen into the dark earthen pits of fashion.

feygele from the german vögelein meaning "little bird."

little bird, where do you flame from?

where do you bird from little german flame?

little singlet split for entry. little finger slipped

into the mouth staring hard across the bare wet bar.

little bear in his arrogant leather harness, his broad

american faith. carry me with you across the fleshless

threshold how an old woman carries her language

across an ocean so vast, so many fathoms deep

one might imagine all life springing from the wet

slit of its shoreline. sure i've memorized every word

for faggot & nearly all their origins are plural & bound

together with twine. little string corset wrapped

around my brothers' thighs. little horses wild

at the bit to be ridden. little films where the animals

are let out but only at night. sure i've eaten directly

from the hand of a man who taught me the simplest

words, gestures of thirst & begging. sure i was hatched

into a world that expected me to fly straight into power-

lines. but see how hideous hearse-shined my feathers,

see my wings spread like a dead book of legs,

see my brutal beak a seed-thief in the club light.

my first name was flame & i drew moths & mouths alike.

feygele as in son of the first preacher with gills. as in

the flood that began & refused to quench. as in when

i was a child i killed a bird, sparrow i think, with my bare

hands so it wouldn't go on suffering, it was sick.

give me your hands, hold my skull between them

how you'd hold a bag writhing with birds, a pillowcase

thick with lights, two grown boys in gowns howling,

a cold mud village consumed by flames, a cage door

opening, a blade, a blade, ablaze.

Butthole

o putrid rose. o floral gift from some dead god
i buried alive only to excavate and find, still fresh.

o myriad sweet sounds i make with it: trumpet,
trombone, tornado, goblin. o second mouth

that gapes and swallows. o second mouth that hungers
for new tongue. o stomach that rests so far from

the colon but still calls him cousin. o come, o old
world magic, o small hungry prince.

how many octaves can you tuba? how many eloquent
speeches come right from the gut? what countless

phallic shapes have you named husband? what knuckle
tucked into you, a dyke holding up all this stale water.

sweet you who birthed iron when i took too many
women's multivitamins claiming there's no such thing

as gender. praise, how you expand and shrink like
a house's water pipes. praise, how when you bleed

you're always trying to tell me something. praise you,
tiny gymnast. beast with a breathing halo.

gold band that weds my strange body to this strange
strange earth.

Sam Sax

Epithalamium

A kiss. Train ride home from a late dinner,
City Hall and document signing. Wasn't cold
but we cuddled in an empty car, legal.
Last month a couple of guys left a gay bar
and were beaten with poles on the way
to their car. No one called them faggot
so no hate crime's documented. A beat down
is what some pray for, a pulse left to count.
We knew we weren't protected. We knew
our rings were party favors, gold to steal
the shine from. We couldn't protect us,
knew the law wouldn't know how. Still, his
beard across my brow, the burn of his cologne.
When the train stopped, the people came on.

Final Poem for Grandma Elizabeth's Cancer

Can I have this dance, White Light, you old worn
and loose-lip gossip? You say it's time.
No. My grandson has to rub my feet first.
Can't break tradition for a little Death
eager to get on with his business. Give
respect to the ones you take. Be patient

'cause I ain't rushing. I've been patient
and bed-rested to tears. Hiding these worms
nobody call hair no more. Can you give
Constance, my daughter, a dream? Warn her time's
eating itself to the bone to stall death.
Rest awhile with me, Old Light. I'll go first

call of the sparrow tomorrow morn. First
answer me this. Am I cute? Greg was patient
netting this wig on his mama's bald death.
Can't look all that bad. Spent hours warring
eagerly with what's left of my hair. Time
rocked in that corner, quiet. What you give?

Could you rub my cold, stiff feet for me? Give
a final shock to my toes. Veins left first,
nook-and-crannied into varicose. Thyme,
chamomile, and spearmint oil patiently
eased on each heel. Rub it in, now. Yes. Worm
right in that spot with your bony thumb. Death,

can I marry you where I'm going? Death-
afraid, my last man had nothing to give.
Not like you, swooping up in here a worn
cyclone all flame-eyed and torn tendon. First
evening a godly man visit, patient.
Rummage in my closet for a shawl. Time

come that I get ready for our date, timed
almost perfectly. I've been so lonely, Death;
nurturing shadows with my breasts. Patience
can wear thin and I hear frail wings giving
early morning their hollow-boned song. First
razor of sun come cutting up my worn,

bloated legs. Patience: I've had it to give.
Yes, now it's time to shed this skin's long death:
empty bedpans, first light breeze. Child, this warmth.

Benjamin Garcia

The Great Glass Closet

This is not a metaphor: when I say that I lived in the closet, it's because I lived in the closet.

You might, too, if you shared a one-bedroom apartment with eleven other people and a pet: mother, stepfather, brother, brother, brother, uncle, aunt, cousin, cousin, cousin, cousin, dog. Then there's me, the surplus.

You could have called our closet a walk-in closet in the sense that a child's body could walk in. Mine did, and I called it home. It was comfortable enough, if you were willing to lie. I was.

//

I lived in a confession booth, listening to my own secrets, making my own sentences.

Confession: my uncle was different in a way you could see.
                I was different in a way you could see

only if you were looking.
      If you were looking, I could see.

What I mean is that my uncle walked on crutches, so he couldn't cross the border by foot. He climbed into the trunk of a car, which is a kind of closet.

I was like my uncle, and I was not like my uncle. He walked on crutches and I didn't.

Confession: during prayers, I don't close my eyes. Nobody knows this except the other people who don't close their eyes.

//

A life in the closet is a life that's closed, so I opened what I could—books. I was Harry Potter, The Boy Who Lived, reading about The Boy Who Lived.

I had no owl, no hat, no wand. I couldn't cast a spell, and I couldn't spell. But I could see the *low* in *owl*, I could pull the *hat* out of *that*, and in the word *wand* find another hidden *and*.

Reading X-Men, I wanted to be Storm so that I could end the famine in my family's village, looking like a badass bitch/queen/goddess doing it. I knew this was impossible because I wasn't claustrophobic enough. I could never be Storm.

I survived too many storms behind a closet door. And I could never change my name to Storm, which at its core contains an *or*. As in, either/or. As in, Ororo Monroe—Storm's birth name.

You must choose:
    pink or blue, boy or girl, left or right, right or wrong, truth or lie, truth or dare.

Truth: even writing this I thought that feminine shared an *a* with famine—*femanine*. Dare: hunger for errors, find another place to stick a *man* inside.

Reading, I learned the difference between *cloth* and *clothe*. Also the difference between *close*, meaning *to shut*, and *close*, meaning *almost there*.

//

Sometimes there's no difference between the past and present, as in: *to read* and *to have read*.

Sometimes there's no difference between the past and present except for the surroundings. You can call this context or you can call this what it is—privilege. Not living in the closet is what people like me did on TV.

But I wasn't like the people on TV, so I lived in the closet.

//

In *Fun Home*, when Alison and her father see a woman wearing men's clothes and sporting a man's haircut, she says:

"Like a traveler from a foreign country who runs into someone from home— someone they've never spoken to, but know by sight—I recognized her with a surge of joy."

"Dad recognized her, too."

Spoiler alert: Alison and her father were both in the closet, but they were not in the closet together.

//

My room was a closet for my family's clothes, my clothes were a closet for my skin, my skin is a closet for my skeleton. It won't always be.

It won't always be this way,

but that's not the same as "it gets better."

Better requires context:

a shell could be a spent bullet or the home of a mollusk.

In order to breathe, you have to add the little snail of an *e* to the end of the word *breath*.

//

It's nothing amazing, but in the closet is where I first read *The Voyages of Doctor Doolittle*. Marooned on Spider Monkey Island, the only way Tommy can go home is to climb inside the pink shell of the Great Glass Sea Snail.

I lived in the closet—all wall, no window. So that if I turned out the light, it made no difference if I shut my eyes. That's how dark it got.

I used to pretend I was Tommy inside the enormous shell—all window, no wall. But what was there to see at the bottom of the sea? Nothing except rare animals that learned, under great pressure, to make light from nothing but the nothing that they are.

It was cold down there. And lonely. My breath would fog the shell until I wiped it clear.

But I climbed in when the the Great Glass Sea Snail bowed its great neck to me and let me enter, hoping I had enough air, heading straight for whatever waited on the next shore,

      like any immigrant would.

Richie Hofmann

Book of Statues

Because I am a boy, the untouchability of beauty
is my subject already, the book of statues
open in my lap, the middle of October, leaves
foiling the wet ground
in soft copper. "A statue
must be beautiful
from all sides," Cellini wrote in 1558.
When I close the book,
the bodies touch. In the west,
they are tying a boy to a fence and leaving him to die,
his face unrecognizable behind a mask
of blood. His body, icon
of loss, growing meaningful
against his will.

The Antiquities

I am on foot, getting lost in the town where my brother
and sister were born, where my mother
and my father met in high school, where my grandmother
and my grandfather met in high school. I want so shamelessly to belong
to someone hairy and popular.
Even though it is dark, I love
the lit interiors I walk by: the other worlds
transpiring inside them—the Ralph Lauren dining rooms,
faces on flat-screen TVs. In one house, there's a jowly dog in a cone
that looks like an Orthodox ikon.
The idea of my homonormative life is far off.
A kid in a passing car shouts something terrible
and he is right.

Joshua Jennifer Espinoza

It Doesn't Matter if I'm Understood

You'll still try to destroy me in your own way

Maybe with your hands
Maybe with your silence
Maybe with your tacit approval of this machine

Here us women are
crackling like sparklers above a lawn
scraping diamonds from asphalt
giving praise to the mountains before us

Our love and our grace and our tenderness
enough to change the shape of the universe

You say goddess or you say dead girl
We live in the margins but don't get a taste
of the joy of being there

Not without loss
Not without broken bones and bandaged flesh

Our condition is nameless
and we know this
so we drift and deflate and let the wind have us

but we don't stop living
even when we sense our impending ghost
even when we finger the dirt and think home

Our life was always a thing of magic
and magic is what lives outside of law

One day we will be allowed to exist
and you will never see us again

It Is Important To Be Something

This is like a life. This is lifelike.
I climb inside a mistake
and remake myself in the shape
of a better mistake—
a nice pair of glasses
without any lenses,
shoes that don't quite fit,
a chest that always hurts.
There is a checklist of things
you need to do to be a person.
I don't want to be a person
but there isn't a choice,
so I work my way down and
kiss the feet.
I work my way up and lick
the knee.
I give you my skull
to do with whatever you please.
You grow flowers from my head
and trim them too short.
I paint my nails nice and pretty
and who cares. Who gives a shit.
I'm trying not to give a shit
but it doesn't fit well on me.
I wear my clothes. I wear my body.
I walk out in the grass and turn red
at the sight of everything.

Marcelo Hernandez Castillo

First Gesture in Reverse

I am lying on the floor
in a pair of blue panties
that I borrowed
without telling.

Here I spread open
and become the knife
with its large smile
tilted away.

This is a star,
and this is a star.

I am thirsty.
It's called unbuckling.

I could be a bride.
Can you see it?
Aren't I a doll?

Here are my lips.
Here is the rain,
and the sound
they are capable of
inside each other.

Here the mirror
through which
I am unbearable.

The brown boy
waving the flag
of his father.

the brown boy
kissing the floor back.

If I can still close,
I will let the rain finish
what the light began
and never tell
anyone about it.

Esparto, California

Each pepper field is the same.
            In each one I am a failed anthem.

I don't know English
            but there is so little
            that needs to be translated.

For twelve hours I have picked
the same colored pepper.
Still I don't know what country
does death belong to.

My skin is peeling.
Cual dios quisiera ser fuente?

If only I could choose what hurt.
An inheritance.
            Those lost mothers bound
            to the future of their blood.

I am walking again through the footage
where the white dress loses its shape.

Even moving my hands to sort
the peppers is a kind of running.
Hold still.
The child will sing because I was once her flag.

            She will take my picture
            —both groom and bride—
            a country she has never seen.

I will give her the knife
to make her own camera.
The gift of shade and water—
          the likeness of a star to possess.

And I am only half sick if being sick
is just a bone waiting to harden.

I could be a saint since there exists no pleasure
that wasn't first abandoned to us out of boredom.
We traffic in the leftovers of ecstasy.

How lonely and inventive those angels were.
          If I could speak their language,
I would tell them all my real name
          —*Antonia*—

And with my curved knife,
I would rid them of all their failures.

Jonah Mixon-Webster

Black Hauntology No 6: *The Hang Around Blues*

ain't nun to do but hang around
ain't nun to do but hang around
and I ain't got no way
to make it out
tried to find me some help
know it can't be found

so ain't nun to do but hang around
ain't nuttin to do but hang around
ain't even got me a penny
to make a pound
they bout took all I had
who am I now?

well ain't nun to do but hang around
ain't nun to do but hang out
if I could I'll run right
straight outta town
don't even need me no shoes
just feet on the ground

now ain't nun to do but hang around
ain't nun to do but hang around
ain't no new news
to think about
so I'ma tell you later
and I'ma tell you now

that ain't nun to do but hang around
ain't nun to do but hang around
now imagine if they never
woulda cut me down

say imagine if they never
woulda cut me down

I would have made it out (no question)
still be found
feet on the ground
outta town
coulda took a penny
and make a pound
out of water
and underground
said I tell you now
that I'd still be found
said I tell you now
that I'd still be found

Black Martyrdom No 6: *Litany of the Spectacle*

Come guillotine. Come gallows. Come gas soaked pyre.
Come charred jaw. Come hot pike. Come hoary beast.
Come ardent hunger. Come garrote wire. Come death
wizard. Come adze. Come axe. Come taut rope. Come
head knot, neck kink. Come click-clack. Come firing
hammer. Come clank. Come bullet. Come wet smoke.
Come slump body, bloody brook. Come bloated excision.
Come slung wrist. Come wind rot. Come dead relic.
Come unholy witness, onlooker lens. Come click, click,
click, CLICK-CLACK-CLANK. Come bullet.
Come bullet. Come bullet. Come
bullet. Come bullet. Bullet.
Bullet. Bullet. Bullet. Bullet.
Bullet. Bullet. Bullet. Bullet.
Bullet. Bullet. Bullet. Pull it. Pull
it. Pull it. Pull it. Pull it. Pull it.
Pull it. Pull it. Pull it. Pull it. Pull

Jonah Mixon-Webster

Ocean Vuong

Threshold

In the body, where everything has a price,
        I was a beggar. On my knees,

I watched, through the keyhole, not
        the man showering, but the rain

falling through him: guitar strings snapping
        over his globed shoulders.

He was singing, which is why
        I remember it. His voice—

it filled me to the core
        like a skeleton. Even my name

knelt down inside me, asking
        to be spared.

He was singing. It is all I remember.
        For in the body, where everything has a price,

I was alive. I didn't know
        there was a better reason.

That one morning, my father would stop
        —a dark colt paused in downpour—

& listen for my clutched breath
        behind the door. I didn't know the cost

of entering a song—was to lose
        your way back.

So I entered. So I lost.
    I lost it all with my eyes

wide open.

Telemachus

Like any good son, I pull my father out
of the water, drag him by his hair

through white sand, his knuckles carving a trail
the waves rush in to erase. Because the city

beyond the shore is no longer
where we left it. Because the bombed

cathedral is now a cathedral
of trees. I kneel beside him to show how far

I might sink. *Do you know who I am,
Ba?* But the answer never comes. The answer

is the bullet hole in his back, brimming
with seawater. He is so still I think

he could be anyone's father, found
the way a green bottle might appear

at a boy's feet containing a year
he has never touched. I touch

his ears. No use. I turn him
over. To face it. The cathedral

in his sea-black eyes. The face
not mine—but one I will wear

to kiss all my lovers good-night:
the way I seal my father's lips

with my own & begin
the faithful work of drowning.

Jos Charles

from *feeld*

XXVIII.

pockes in the pewtre agayn / gashe inn that sintacks /
a tran / her nayme sum flynt all redey inn the ash /
i cant stop riting tran / her dubble nayme / the boyes
cull inn 2 a nachurl rowe / the guarden they flaten wen
they pas / 2 wut / this mornygne / i saw u / a bel spilt
inn a feeld / onlie ther was no feeld / & a catheedril is
not its bel / but sum wringynge / no nayme but 2
wrecken with the wringynge / mye breasthes grone / a
bel i tend / & its stunnynge / a thynge / before its gone

XLV.

but wen i was a chylde / i was so olde / inn my dreems
/ a grl / ther bieng no pardon / from the reel / its form
a dreem / a grl / the feeld is an æffekt yes / but wut
mattres more / than its fakt / faktual the folde / inn its
fallow / & bent daye / mattrynge / how wee call a
thynge / & wut / did wee make then / being so tall /
the daye bieng olde / sum fakts / stunnynge the aire

Kaveh Akbar

A Boy Steps into the Water

and of course he's beautiful
goosebumps over his ribs
like tiny fists under a thin sheet   the sheet
all mudwet and taste of walnut

and of course I'm afraid of him
of the way keeping him a secret will make him
inevitable   I will do anything to avoid
getting carried away   sleep nightly with coins

over my eyes   set fire to an entire
zodiac   mecca is a moth
chewing holes in a shirt I left
at a lover's house   a body loudly

consumes days and awaits the slow
fibrillation of its heart   a lightning rod
sits in silence until finally   the storm
now the boy is scooping up minnows

and swallowing them like a heron
I'm done trying to make sense
of any of this   no one will believe anything
that comes out a mouth like mine

Some Boys Aren't Born They Bubble

some boys aren't born they bubble
        up from the earth's crust   land safely around
kitchen tables green globes of fruit already

           in their mouths   when they find themselves crying
     they stop crying these boys moan
        more than other boys   they do as desire

demands   when they dance their bodies plunge
      into space and recover   the music stays
in their breastbones they sing songs about

        storms then dry their shoes on porches
    these boys are so cold their pilot lights never light
        they buy the best heat money can buy   blue flames

swamp smoke   they are desperate
     to lick and be licked   sometimes one will eat
all the food in a house or break every bone

        in his jaw   sometimes one will disappear into himself
   like a ram charging a mirror when this happens
      they all feel it   afterwards the others dream

of rain their pupils boil they light black candles
     and pray the only prayer they know   *oh lord*
spare this body   *set fire to another*

Franny Choi

Upon Learning That Some Korean War Refugees Used Partially Detonated Napalm Canisters as Cooking Fuel

Somewhere is a prior world, a woman with my face
is scraping the seeds from an unborn hell.
All night, doom rang from the sky. And in the morning,
there are mouths to feed. There are crocks in the cellar
and the ruined crops, the early frost, the neighbor's red daughter
strung up in the square. What else to do
when the unspeakable comes. What to burn
when it doesn't. Somewhere in a world that didn't quite
end, a woman like me is foraging for that which failed to kill her.
She is cranking open modernity's throat, wrenching
her arc from its scat. She is a woman who can hack
an impossible morning into water, bean paste, bitter leaves,
another chance to fumble toward the next chance, and the next—
Every day of my life has been something other than my last.
Every day, an extinction misfires, and I put it to work.

Rememory

Atlanta / Seoul / Kwangju

Whose story was I remembering when riot cops closed in
on all four sides, and a sound happened from somehow me?

The sound was a sound from 1980—year my father was a young man.
Year of bayonets; year of soldiers shooting into crowds, limbs on fire.

My father was a student of biology in another year of martial law,
in a century of war. Bayonet of interruption—my father touched diagrams,

threw rocks at riot gear and wondered what for. It was another year
when they shut the school gates, and students died in the street.

The crowds were gassed and ran choking from the scene.
This year, someone else's father is a young man, choking, and the crowds

are gassed, and we run, boots on the ground. I remember:
this night, this year; no route out of the cops' kettle; me in the crowd,

shouting Americanly until the cops study forward with their shields
and fists and then, someone unremembered inside me is wailing; wailing;

someone else's song crawling backwards from my mouth. Whose song:
Hell of looking. Bodies in a heap. Mother-shrieks in white hemp.

Boots on the ground—boots? on the bloody ground? Whose voice was that.
Whose year is it. *Whose streets.* This city, this *our*—slow bayonet of claiming,

whose tank in my mouth? Bayonet of this: American me, fathering nothing
but the wails of strangers I'll never caress. Bayonet of dispersal, gas.

We run, choking on the sound of century and century's return.
I run, and a country breaks its way out of me, then breaks, breaks.

Chen Chen

Summer

You are the ice cream sandwich connoisseur of your generation.

Blessed are your floral shorteralls, your deeply pink fanny pack with travel-size lint roller just in case.

Level of splendiferous in your outfit: 200.

Types of invisible pain stemming from adolescent disasters in classrooms, locker rooms, & quite often Toyota Camrys: at least 10,000.

You are not a jigglypuff, not yet a wigglytuff.

Reporters & fathers call your generation "the worst."

Which really means "queer kids who could go online & learn that queer doesn't have to mean disaster."

Or dead.

Instead, queer means, splendiferously, you.

& you means someone who knows that common flavors for ice cream sandwiches in Singapore include red bean, yam, & honeydew.

Your powers are great, are growing.

One day you will create an online personality quiz that also freshens the breath.

The next day you will tell your father, *You were wrong to say that I had to change.*

To make me promise I would. To make me promise.

& promise.

I Invite My Parents to a Dinner Party

In the invitation, I tell them for the seventeenth time
(the fourth in writing), that I am gay.

In the invitation, I include a picture of my boyfriend
& write, *You've met him two times. But this time,*

you will ask him things other than can you pass the
whatever. You will ask him

about him. You will enjoy dinner. You will be
enjoyable. Please RSVP.

They RSVP. They come.
They sit at the table & ask my boyfriend

the first of the conversation starters I slip them
upon arrival: *How is work going?*

I'm like the kid in *Home Alone*, orchestrating
every movement of a proper family, as if a pair

of scary yet deeply incompetent burglars
is watching from the outside.

My boyfriend responds in his chipper way.
I pass my father a bowl of fish ball soup—*So comforting,*

isn't it? My mother smiles her best
Sitting with Her Son's Boyfriend

Who Is a Boy Smile. I smile my Hurray for Doing
a Little Better Smile.

Everyone eats soup.
Then, my mother turns

to me, whispers in Mandarin, *Is he coming with you
for Thanksgiving? My good friend is & she wouldn't like*

this. I'm like the kid in *Home Alone*, pulling
on the string that makes my cardboard mother

more motherly, except she is
not cardboard, she is

already, exceedingly my mother. Waiting
for my answer.

While my father opens up
a *Boston Globe*, when the invitation

clearly stated: *No security
blankets.* I'm like the kid

in *Home Alone*, except the home
is my apartment, & I'm much older, & not alone,

& not the one who needs
to learn, has to—*Remind me*

what's in that recipe again, my boyfriend says
to my mother, as though they have always, easily

talked. As though no one has told him
many times, what a nonlinear slapstick meets

slasher flick meets psychological
pit he is now co-starring in.

Remind me, he says
to our family.

Remembering God After Three Years of Depression

Where were your rough, familiar hands
smelling of rosemary? Insomnia watched me,
wild-haired and unwashed, like an officer.
Perhaps the light through the keyhole
was you, floorboards straining in another room.
In the hall, a sleepwalker sang the blues,
bleeding dream into the world.
I feared a knock at the door. I needed a hand.
Would you have found me on the deflated air
mattress, among filthy shirts, half-eaten food?
I don't know what to call doubt when you are here
and I am not. What is it to be exiled in you?
Maybe if I'd been drinking red instead of white.
I had no space in me for less than life.

Exegesis as Self-Elegy

Mark 14:51–52

Remember the boy watching soldiers enter a garden

> (Before the bullets, before I bled out
> on the concrete under an American
> sun, I loved white roses.)

where the mind cannot imagine more

> (There's a snowbank
> of roses on the sidewalk
> where America unmade me.)

than what it sees and flesh is transfigured

> (We cannot say this
> is not an old story.)

and made guilty by bonds alone,

> (The state is always afraid.)

where the disciples mourned and the boy was loved,

> (An education may begin
> with the scent of olive trees
> or busted Heineken bottles
> greening the air.)

where he scorched the night with his blackness and lived.

Derrick Austin

In the Decadence of Silence

after Diedrick Brackens's exhibition darling divined

I saw once, at the black sand beach, men coming out of the sea,
Black men coming into and out of the sea,

as if they were looking for something, grace maybe, something harsh and small
as the grains of black sand that fell from my clothes for weeks,

and those men were not vexed in their looking
and seemed happy, blissful even, in their gorgeous company.

A dolphin lept from the water. Gulls piped up. Freighters in distant fog.
I was born under the sign of anxiety and pleasure.

All I cared for was the men's laughter and the way one reached
for the hand of another coming ashore, the stretch when sand pulls at your feet

and the rough surf is against you. They held each other by the waist.
They teased and shoved. They wiped salt from each other's eyes.

One man returned with a cup and seeing me alone
offered it, beckoned with that sea-saved chalice.

And it must have been filled with salt water. And it must have been
a bitter, grainy drink. And it must have been good, like joy.

It would drive me to madness to live on it. From the cliffs
the gods of death and desire watched. But they were not gods.

They were palm trees, dark and still,
until they leaned east in the wind and then were still again.

Dorothy Chan

Straight Girls

The girls I knew at eighteen would make fun of me
For eating a cheeseburger and caramel shake
At midnight. I wonder about the fixation some women
Have on how men perceive their figures—
I wonder about the fixation men have on women's bodies—
By these standards, no one will ever be pretty.
Have you ever met the hot wife and the man who let himself
Go simply by virtue of being a man. Ironic. I wonder
What it would be like to walk around the world all big and male
And white and over six feet tall. I wonder how many people
Would throw themselves at me, let me get away with
The biggest and smallest crimes. The girls I knew at eighteen
Would make fun of me for eating a cheeseburger
And caramel shake at midnight. In Chinese culture, we show
Our love through food: the slurping of soup and noodles,
Or how when I attended a friend's birthday party
At nine, my parents went home with fish parts her parents
Didn't want to use. I ate every part of the animal growing up.
My brother and I don't get along, but when we're eating
Pigs' ears, we're like two childhood best friends.
As a teenager in Hong Kong, my mother loved eating
Red bean gelatin long after dinner. The girls I knew at eighteen
Would make fun of me for eating a cheeseburger
And caramel shake at midnight. They giggled over jerk boys.
I wonder about the white girls I saw at EPCOT
Trying on Qipao, trying on kimonos, not knowing the difference.
I felt bad for the East Asian women who had to serve them.
I think these white women wanted to look like movie stars—
Like Hollywood celebrities on the red carpet with chopsticks
In their hair. I think about my mother's stubby toe,
A symbol of Chinese suffering—the way she's always put
My happiness and my father's over hers.

Triple Sonnet, Because She Makes Me Hot

She makes me hot, so I eat chocolate cheesecake
after our phone call, down an espresso, and take
    a hot shower, because it's one of those nights
I've craved since I was a little girl who
    discovered that boys weren't the only option,
and I remember my first crushes on women—
    the fantasy of starring in my own trashy
mid 2000s reality show on MTV where
    it's a double (or triple)
                    shot at love,
and I'd strut around in emerald lingerie,
    telling the boys and girls to spank me,
feed me carrot cake, and go out for a midnight
    swim in the nude. And isn't it sexy how often
water appears in our dreams? But of course,

        not all love is trashy, and I think about
    dressing up in a cheerleader costume,
        telling the lady contestants, I used to sneak
a glimpse of the girls on the football field.
        But I'd rather skip gym class, paint all over
canvases with beauties, or be ambitious, like
        Tara Reid's Vicky in *American Pie*, looking
oh, so fine in her gray Cornell t-shirt, and
        it's oh so tight, Tara, and isn't it ironic
how I ended up going Big Red, or back
        to my college days in Ithaca when my friend
L and I would tongue under my covers,
        saying "This is practice for the boys,"
but we knew what we were doing—*How*

does one even achieve intimacy?
        is really the million-dollar question
of the century, and L, what we had
        wasn't a phase, and I remember donning
your yellow flannel after the sun went down
        in those Ithaca winters, and how you'd
eye me saying, "You look like you just
        had sex," and we'd laugh and hug and I'd walk
home. And sometimes I feel frozen in that
        moment in time, when I'd get home, crawl
into my own bed, in the nude, thinking about
        my friend Anna's words, "I think girls in boyish
clothes look more feminine," and I'd wipe off
        my red lipstick with a tissue—fall asleep.

Dorothy Chan

Catherine Pond

I'm a Young Cowboy and Know I've Done Wrong

I'm a young cowboy and know I've done wrong,
my father sang as I emerged from the river.

She likes wearing men's clothes, let her wear them,
said my mother, tying his denim shirt around my neck.

Under the surface of the water, rocks glimmered
like small hearts. Here's the mountain

where we stood in order of height, stars flashing
across our faces. What my father could not give my mother

she gave to herself. I wanted to be like that;
like the lawnmower, commanding respect, a steady echo.

Instead I was more like the grass, in love
with being severed, and later, with finding those parts

of myself that had been buried, thin blades
only the fresh spring rain had the power to recover.

Tatiana

White taffeta circled her waist
looped with a thin brown belt. I reached out and slid
my hand under. Don't,
she said. We're sisters.

Outside the castle, the kingdom
fluttered apart. Blues and reds and golds
bled out against the snow. Our mother

had lost her mind. She had found
religion. At night I watched through the keyhole
as she lowered herself
in front of the bearded starets. I didn't know about
sex. I was in love

with my sister.
This was before Tsarskoye Selo,
before Yekaterinburg,
before I watched her body drop
into my lap like a piece
of driftwood, all that dark hair
against my hand.

Carolina Prayer

Let the blood if your belly must have it, but let it
not be of me and mine. Let my momma sleep.
Let her pray. Let them eat. Let the reverend's
devil pass over me. Let the odds at least
acknowledge us. Let the breasts be intact,
the insulin faithfully not far, and let the deep
red pinpoint puddle its urgency on a pricked
fingertip. Let the nurse find the vein the first time.

Let the kerosene flow and let my grandma praise
her bedside lord for letting her miss another winter.
Let me be just a little bit bitter so I remember:
Your columns and borders aint but the fractured,
the broke clean, the brownest gouges in the blades
of our great-great-great-shoulders. Let me leave
and come back when my chest opens for you wider
than your ditches did to engorge my placeless body.

The mosquito-thick breath in your throat coats my skin
and it almost feels as if you love me. Let the AC
drown out the TV. Let the lotion bottle keep a secret
corner til Friday. Let Ike, Wan, D-Block, all my brother's
brothers ride through the weekend. Let the cop car
swerve its nose into night and not see none of them.
Let us smell rain. Let the breeze through an oak hymn
the promise that keeps us waking. Let the cicada
unwind while hushpuppy steam slips out the knot
of a tourist's hand, and let him hear in it legends
of how hot grease kept the hounds and the lash at bay.

Beneficence

If I want them dead
I don't mean the kind of dead
my momma will be

which I prepare to swear
is like, after standing
in a night so calm

it cuts the line of nights before
and after it in two
like Christ's birth

is said to,
handing such a night
to the world's other hemisphere.

        I suppose I don't
wish death on them. I don't wish them
on anyone

but themselves. One day
I'll have to come to terms
for who and what it is

I mean by *them*
and risk having my mind changed
about them, as I have

risked being just as reductive as they
have become *they*
by being.

I expect that
on such a day when my momma is dead
I will want

to be able to stand
beneath whatever sky
is left to me

and offer kindness
even to them and,
in unfolding both my hands

to offer this—
side by side as if to let fly
some fragile-winged sentience—

experience my two hands
mended into a single tenderness,
meridianless,

and all the lightning bugs
continuing to be,
then not be, then be elsewhere

greenly in the black night.
I suppose yes
yes I'll want to be this way.

Danez Smith

fall poem

the leaves done done their annual shimmy.
now the streetlight with no soft green curtain
cuts a silver blade across my bed

& my body. i didn't want to start with leaves
even though i love how the trees turn the color of aunts
& soul-train-line to the ground each October. no one

wants to hear a poem about fall; much prefer the fallen
body, something easy to mourn, body cut out of the light
body lit up with bullets. see how easy it is to bring up bullets?

is it possible to ban guns? even from this poem?
i lie in the light, body split by light, room too bright for sleep
thinking of the leaf-colored bodies, their weekly fall

how their bodies look like mounds of a tree's shed skin
a child could jump into them & play for hours.
there i go, talking about our dead & if you don't think

they are your dead, i've run from your hands. they are red
like the tree down the street, a hot-air balloon
of blood, the leaves dyed fruit-punch red, red as a child's red mouth

after an afternoon spent on the porch with a bag of takis
watching other kids walk by, waiting for kids who don't
pass anymore on the other side of summer, who maybe go

to a different school or moved out east or made like a tree
& now sleep in a box made from one.

say it with your whole black mouth

say it with your whole black mouth: i am innocent.
& if you are not innocent, say this: i am worthy

of forgiveness, of breath after breath.
i tell you this: i let blue eyes dress me in guilt

walked around stores convinced the very skin
of my palm was stolen. what good has it brought?

days filled flinching thinking the sirens
were reaching for me. & when the sirens were mine

did i not make peace with God?
so many white people are alive

because we know how to control ourselves.
how many times have we died on a whim

wielded like gallows in their sun-shy hands?
here, standing in my own body, i say: the next time

they murder us for the crime of their imaginations
i don't know what i'll do.

i did not come to preach of peace
for that's not the hunted's duty.

i came here to say what i can't say
without my name being added to a list

what my mother fears i will say
what she wishes to say herself

i came here to say

i can't bring myself to write it down

sometimes i dream of pulling an apology
from a pig's collared neck & wake up crackin' up

if i dream of setting fire to cul-de-sacs
i wake chained to the bed

i don't like thinking about doing to white folks
what white folks done to us

when i do

        can't say

    i don't dance

o my people

    how long will we

reach for God

    instead of something

      sharper?

         Danez Smith

Cameron Awkward-Rich

Faggot Poetics

> *Yet I was, in peculiar truth, a very lucky boy.*
> —*James Baldwin*

In any case, the story begins
with darkness. A classroom.

A broom closet. A bowl of bruised
light held over a city. Or the story

begins with a child playing
the role of an ashy plum—

how it rises to meet the man's teeth
or doesn't. How the skin is broken

or breaks because the body just wants
what it wants: to be a hallway

where men hang their photos
on the wall. Does that make sense?

To want to own the image of the man
but not the man? To bask in that memory

of what first nailed you to the dark?

Cento Between the Ending and the End

Sometimes you don't die

when you're supposed to

& now I have a choice

repair a world or build

a new one inside my body

a white door opens

into a place queerly brimming

gold light so velvet-gold

it is like the world

hasn't happened

when I call out

all my friends are there

everyone we love

is still alive gathered

at the lakeside

like constellations

my honeyed kin

honeyed light

beneath the sky

a garden blue stalks

white buds the moon's

Cameron Awkward-Rich

marble glow the fire

distant & flickering

the body whole brightwinged brimming

with the hours

of the day beautiful

nameless planet. Oh

friends, my friends—

bloom how you must, wild

until we are free.

Michael Wasson

A Boy & His Mother Play Dead at Dawn

The presence of mothers and babies in the blue
rifle smoke that made dawn more dim.
            —C.E.S. Wood, 1884

Tucked beneath
        a bank of brush.
Held between my legs
        are my hands.
Like prayer.
        Like holding in
my morning piss.
        & I do. It's warmer
at the lip's edge
        of pink water. Is it
the dead we're about
        to become?
She dunks me
        beneath. Purpled
ripples erasing me.
        Some hunched men
check the grounds
        for skulls. Some
will drag the dead us
        to the open mouth
of the creek. & of
        course they smell
me. She nods:
        cepée'yehey'ckse
I'll make you
        soft by soaking,
my son when she floods
        around me. I pull in

my tongue from any
        taste. We flower
from the inside out.
        Please don't mistake
her for another now.
        I'm still. Dawn
mirrored then crushed
        by another hidden rain
of hollowed gunmetal.
        This slow-motion
massacre crowding
        silenced. Each body
pressing her freed weight
        into me. Mouth
agape. *teqúuse 'iin. This*
        warmth. Drown
me I beg no one. Hurry.
        Empty me out.   .

This Dusk in a Mouth Full of Prayer

When you first came
                          into my mouth
              opened wide enough

to forget
                          how to swallow

light: this surrendering

                          the body is my skin

tracing starved beauty
                          in climax: *us*

lying in the dark
                          shadow of another
              lord: give me your dying

words like *father*
                          or *my tongue*

disappearing before
                          you: welík'ipckse
so tell me this

when you've forgotten
                          how to open

your lips into my name—

                          father: which is
another way to say *shadow:*

failed daylight
               you say: *the sky*

touching the body: I
                 find myself entering

a night again wounded
               enough for the snow—

shined with moon
       —to reorder the stars with
our faces: broken

          through with so many

American mouths: like
               ghosts singing

the very last bright word they

remember: *amen.*

Jake Skeets

How to Become the Moon

He enters you, hide him, a silver dollar
                    beneath your pillow,

in a pawnshop, lodged in your throat. Your birthmark
will remind him of bruising, his father's belt, broom,

branch across his face. He will see his past in the whorl
                                        of your hair

as you go down on him. He sees a boy, afraid of the deep end,
drowning in the swimming pool of your throat.
                            He swears your eyes are chlorine
                blue and black, both of you purple soot.

He says *swallow* but do not,
            hold it as a secret

                            and kiss him
        so he can know you know him

                        the way he can know him, a dark
moon rising from the pool water.
        The lights ribboned on his cheek
as he comes up for air.

The Indian Capital of the World

man hit by train
man found dead possibly from exposure in a field
woman hit by semitruck attempting to cross freeway
woman found dead in arroyo
man hit walking across road
man found dead near train tracks
man found in tunnel
man found in arroyo
man was picked up by two other men then killed
man left in field with stab wound overnight
woman crushed to death by semitruck while asleep in alleyway
woman dead from hit and run
man found murdered and dead in homeless camp
man found dead in a field
man found dead in a field
man found dead in a field
man found dead in a field
man found dead in a field
man found dead in a field
man found dead in a field
man found dead in a field
       dogs mauled his remains
            in the fields
          in the fields in the fields
         in the fields
            field   fields
                fields fields
       fields

           among flowers
             flowers
         among flowers   in the weeds

Christopher Soto

All the Dead Boys Look Like Us

for Orlando

Last time we saw ourselves die is when police killed Jessie Hernandez

      A seventeen-year-old brown queer // Who was sleeping in their car

Yesterday we saw ourselves die again // Fifty times we died in Orlando // &

      We remember reading // Dr. José Esteban Muñoz before he passed

We were studying at NYU // Where he was teaching // Where he wrote shit that

      Made us feel that queer brown survival was possible // But he didn't

Survive & now // On the dancefloor // In the restroom // On the news // In our chest

      There are another // Fifty bodies that look like ours // & Are

Dead // & We've been marching for Black Lives // & Talking about police brutality

      Against Native communities too // For years // But this morning

We feel it // We really feel it again // How can we imagine ourselves // Today

      Black // Native // Brown people // How can we imagine ourselves when

All the dead boys look like us // Once we asked our nephew where he wanted

      To go to college // What career he wants // As if

The whole world was his for the choosing // Once he answered me without fearing

Tombstones or cages // Or the hands from a father // The hands of our lover

Yesterday praised our whole body // Made angels from my lips // Ave Maria

Full of grace // He propped us up like the roof of a cathedral // In NYC

Before we opened the news & red // & Read about people who think two Brown queers

Can't build cathedrals // Only cemeteries // & Each time we kissed

A funeral plot opens // In the bedroom we accepted his kiss // & We lost our reflection

We're tired of writing this poem // But we wanted to say one last word about

Yesterday // Our father called // We heard him cry for only the second time in our life

He sounded like he loves us // It's something we're rarely able to hear &

We hope // If anything // His sound's what our body remembers first

Christopher Soto   311

The Terrorist Shaved His Beard

after Cecilia Vicuña & Layli Long Soldier

The root of terrorism is terror
      Etymologically derived from
      The Spanish word tierra // Meaning land

Or maybe // The root of terrorism is error
      Etymologically derived from
      The Greek // Err // Meaning to be incorrect

Or maybe we err about the etymology
      Maybe we're wrong // To think terrorism means
      One who exists incorrectly on this land

In Spanish the word terrorism becomes terrorismo
      Terremoto is a slant rhyme // & An earthquake
      A shaking of the land

You change the suffix
      The noun can become a verb // Terrorizing
      For example // Police are terrorizing our people

Or in its past tense // The word becomes // Terrorized
      For example // On this land // Our people were
      Terrorized by police // By ICE

Is it writers only // Who obsess over punctuation
      The question mark // So cute in curiosity
      Question // Who do we call terrorist & why

Christopher Soto

On Crescents & Waning

Just before anesthesia
took me

to the bottom of the ocean,
I looked down my hospital gown

and admired, for the last time,
the fullness of this original body.

My original body had many marvels
but I always wished it for

someone else—spent
years daydreaming of my body

neatly disassembled and sent
to more deserving homes.

But you cannot give oneself
away quite like this.

After the scalpel, my breast tissue
became biological waste.

My body shrunk
to its new original.

Now, under all this
almost-newness,

I watch my own heart as it beats.
I look at my life more

closely than ever, and how beautiful
it is, just under the skin,

alive & alive & alive—
like a warm moon.

Kayleb Rae Candrilli

One Geography of Belonging

after Ocean Vuong

What becomes of the girl
no longer a girl? Dearest Mother,

the stretch marks from my once-breasts
have migrated

to their new tectonic flats.
But you can always find hints

of what used to be. Trust me,
it is more beautiful

this way, to look closely
at my body and name it things like:

Pangea & history & so, so warm.

Look at me now
and see how blood

faithfully takes the shape
of its body,

never asking
too many questions.

Dearest Mother, how many rivers
did I run across your belly?

Do you love
that they will never dry up?

Mother, I'll make all
this water worth it.

Landscape with the Fall of Icarus: Oil on Canvas: Pieter Bruegel the Elder: 1560

Given that the door had to be opened and closed,
the jeans unbuttoned and unzipped, the right hand placed over my mouth
while the left hand held me, held me

there, held me down, I can't help
but think, again then, then and again, that
suffering, its human position, isn't entirely random

because someone has to decide, at some point, with purpose
or not, that they're going to get
what they want or what they tell themselves they want

in order to get what they really want
even if it means hurting another, even if it means hurting them both,
even if they can't discern what they really want

or that they're hurting, yet,
until the hurt and the want, lacking
explanation, or eluding it, become indiscernible

from the rest of their suffering, confused for and eclipsing
that suffering, the way the story of sunlight melting wax wings
is confused for the story of hubris and eclipses the story of the child

following the father, as the child was instructed to,
from one dungeon to another
of sky, and given that, given all that followed

when I followed my father
from our dungeon to one of men
not unlike my father and me, I could've blamed him

for the him who followed, could've maintained the story
that it was neither sunlight nor hubris
that defeated me but descent

while bystanders stood by, and I could've reframed
the defeat as the defect of wings, my descent as my dissent to flight,
and though I did, though I did whenever and however

to suit my schemes, my shifting schema,
I accept, for now, just now, that
in the story it was me, and only me, falling from the sky

to the sea, that as I struggled against my end
I struggled, too, against the fact, falling
and falling, that the end would end, and as I fell

from one blue dungeon to another, I saw
as I fell closer and closer
to the end, the instant preceding the end

when everything could still be changed, in the infinite blue of the water
the infinite blue of the sky
and my face, my father's face and his, looking back.

Bioluminescence

There's a dark so deep beneath the sea the creatures beget their own
light. This feat, this fact of adaptation, I could say, is beautiful

though the creatures are hideous. Lanternfish. Hatchetfish. Viperfish.
I, not unlike them, forfeited beauty to glimpse the world hidden

by eternal darkness. I subsisted on falling matter, unaware
from where or why matter fell, and on weaker creatures beguiled

by my luminosity. My hideous face opening, suddenly, to take them
into a darkness darker and more eternal than this underworld

underwater. I swam and swam toward nowhere and nothing.
I, after so much isolation, so much indifference, kept going

even if going meant only waiting, hovering in place. So far below, so far
away from the rest of life, the terrestrial made possible by and thereby

dependent upon light, I did what I had to do. I stalked. I killed.
I wanted to feel in my body my body at work, working to stay

alive. I swam. I kept going. I waited. I found myself without meaning
to, without contriving meaning at the time, in time, in the company

of creatures who, hideous like me, had to be their own illumination.
Their own god. Their own genesis. Often we feuded. Often we fused

like anglerfish. Blood to blood. Desire to desire. We were wild. Bewildered.
Beautiful in our wilderness and wildness. In the most extreme conditions

we proved that life can exist. *I exist. I am my life,* I thought, approaching
at last the bottom of the sea. It wasn't the bottom. It wasn't the sea.

torrin a. greathouse

All I Ever Wanted to Be Was Nothing at All

I was a shrinking child.   Boy born with an apple
    on her head. Flinching target.

    I learned young to be the smallest bullseye.

How a trans girl's body
            is always down range.

      What better way to vanish   than by mastering
        the stomach's calculus.

My ribs the thin slats of an abacus. Each meal
                an equation.

      My mother used to say that if I just   turned
                    sideways

I would disappear.

                A trick of the light.
The eye glancing off my body   like an arrow off a blade.

    Woman was taught to me
        in a language of subtraction.

So, I skipped meals.
Trimmed fat.

        Dreamed of another body,   revised
      again & again like the rough draft of a coast.

I was always a mouthful away   from unbecoming.

Each calorie
a single match
struck in the gut.

                                          I counted sparks.

Factored out hunger's unnecessary variable.

Swallowed an apple
        like a torch. Slice of pizza
                —a wedge of blistering ore. I Imagined

myself, a wicker girl   trying not to burn.

                I will not say the word
                      scorching both our tongues.

Will not let this become another metaphor

        for how my family taught me
            my body as another name for pyre.

On Using the Wo|men's Bathroom

I open the door &

step onto cold linoleum
wonder who will notice
the stain of stubble
blue skin & wide-set jaw
ignore the swell of new-
born breasts & the mechanism
of these well-trained hips.
Wonder who will see a man
despite the woman of me
& fear my body out of prey.
Make hunger from the implication
of each white tooth.
Imagine herself red meat
my painted face a coyote's skull
turning in on itself.

step out of my own skin
wonder who will imagine
these lips rouged
by their own rough pulse
like an eye's own orbit
can shadow itself Prussian blue
beneath a well-trained fist.
Wonder who will see a man
dressed in woman's clothing
& decide my body a crime
himself a fitting punishment.
Gender of curled fist
I am born of abandoning.
I am only ever woman enough
to become a guilty victim.

I cannot conceive of a different ending
both doors open   both doors open
to a narrative ending in blood.

torrin a. greathouse

Index of Poets

Biographies

SAMUEL ACE is a trans/genderqueer poet and sound artist. His most recent books are *Our Weather Our Sea*; *Meet Me There: Normal Sex; Home in three days. Don't wash.*; and the chapbook *What started / this mess*. Ace is the recipient of the Astraea Lesbian Writer Award and the Firecracker Alternative Book Award in Poetry, as well as a repeat finalist for both the Lambda Literary Award and the National Poetry Series. A book-length poetic essay, *I Want to Start by Saying*, is forthcoming from the Cleveland State University Poetry Center.

KAVEH AKBAR is the author of *Pilgrim Bell*, *Calling a Wolf a Wolf*, and the chapbook *Portrait of the Alcoholic*. He is the editor of *The Penguin Book of Spiritual Verse: 100 Poets on the Divine*. In 2024, his first novel, *Martyr!*, will be published. The recipient of multiple honors, including Pushcart Prizes, a Civitella Ranieri Foundation Fellowship, and the Levis Reading Prize, Akbar was born in Tehran, Iran, and teaches at the University of Iowa and in the low-residency MFA programs at Randolph College and Warren Wilson. In 2014, Kaveh founded *Divedapper*, a home for dialogues with the most vital voices in American poetry. He is Poetry Editor of *The Nation*.

KAZIM ALI was born in the United Kingdom and has lived transnationally in the United States, Canada, India, France, and the Middle East. The author of numerous books encompassing multiple genres, his newest is *Sukun: New and Selected Poems*, and the novel *Indian Winter*. He is also an accomplished translator (of Marguerite Duras, Sohrab Sepehri, Ananda Devi, Mahmoud Chokrollahi, and others) and an editor of several anthologies and books of criticism. He is a Professor of Literature at the University of California, San Diego.

DERRICK AUSTIN is the author of *Tenderness*, winner of the Isabella Gardner Poetry Award, *Trouble the Water*, and the chapbook *Black Sand*. Among his honors are an Amy Lowell Poetry Traveling Scholarship, a Cave Canem fellowship, a Wisconsin Institute of Creative Writing fellowship, and a Stegner Fellowship from Stanford University.

CAMERON AWKWARD-RICH is the author of *Sympathetic Little Monster*, *Dispatch*, and *The Terrible We: Thinking with Trans Maladjustment*. His writing has been supported by fellowships from Cave Canem, the Lannan Foundation, and the American Council of Learned Societies. He is an associate professor in the Department of Women, Gender, Sexuality Studies at the University of Massachusetts, Amherst.

RICK BAROT was born in the Philippines, grew up in the San Francisco Bay Area. He has published four books of poetry, most recently, *The Galleons*, which was listed on the top ten poetry books for 2020 by the New York Public Library, was a finalist for the Pacific Northwest Book Awards, and was on the longlist for the National Book Award. Among his honors are fellowships from the Guggenheim Foundation, the National Endowment for the Arts, the Artist Trust of Washington, the Civitella Ranieri Foundation, and Stanford University; in 2020 Barot received the Shelley Memorial Award from the Poetry Society of America. He lives in Tacoma, Washington, and teaches at Pacific Lutheran University, where he directs The Rainier Writing Workshop, the low-residency MFA in Creative Writing.

ELLEN BASS's most recent collection is *Indigo*. Her other poetry books include *Like a Beggar*, *The Human Line*, and *Mules of Love*. Among her awards are fellowships from the Guggenheim Foundation, the National Endowment for the Arts, The California Arts Council, The Lambda Literary Award, and four Pushcart Prizes. She co-edited the anthology *No More Masks!*, and her nonfiction books include the groundbreaking *The Courage to Heal: A Guide for Women Survivors of Child Sexual Abuse* and *Free Your Mind: The Book for Gay, Lesbian and Bisexual Youth*. A Chancellor Emerita of the Academy of American Poets, Bass founded poetry workshops at Salinas Valley State Prison and the Santa Cruz, California, jails, and teaches in the MFA writing program at Pacific University.

ROBIN BECKER has published six books in the Pitt Poetry Series, most recently *The Black Bear Inside Me*. Seven Kitchens Press holds the annual Robin Becker Chapbook Competition, open to LGBTQ poets, publishing the winning chapbook. Becker has served as Contributing and Poetry Editor of *The Women's Review of Books* and as the Pennsylvania State University Arts Laureate. A collection of Becker's new and selected poems is forthcoming.

MARK BIBBINS is the author of, most recently, *13th Balloon*. His book *They Don't Kill You Because They're Hungry, They Kill You Because They're Full* was named one of the best poetry collections of 2014 by *Publishers Weekly*. He received a Lambda Literary Award for his first book, *Sky Lounge*. Bibbins teaches in the graduate writing programs at Columbia University and The New School, where he co-founded *LIT* magazine, and in New York University's Writers in Florence program.

FRANK BIDART is the author, most recently, of *Against Silence*. His book *Half-light: Collected Poems, 1965–2016* received the Pulitzer Prize and the National Book Award. He has been an English professor at Wellesley College since 1972 and has taught at nearby Brandeis University.

BRIAN BLANCHFIELD is the author, most recently, of *Proxies: Essays Near Knowing*, for which he received a Whiting Award in Nonfiction. His two collections of poetry are *Not Even Then* and *A Several World*, which won the Academy of American Poets' James Laughlin Award. He teaches at the University of Montana and lives with his husband, the poet John Myers, in Missoula.

RICHARD BLANCO was selected by President Obama as the fifth inaugural poet in U.S. history. Born in Madrid to Cuban exile parents and raised in Miami, cultural identity characterizes his many collections of award-winning poetry and prose. Blanco is an associate professor of creative writing at Florida International University and a recent recipient of the National Endowment for the Humanities medal.

TOMMYE BLOUNT is the author of the chapbook *What Are We Not For* and the full-length collection *Fantasia for the Man in Blue*, which was finalist for the National Book Award, the Kate Tufts Discovery Award, the Lambda Literary Award in Gay Poetry, the Hurston/Wright Legacy Award, and others. He is the recipient of commendations, fellowships, and grants from the Whiting Foundation, Cave Canem, Bread Loaf Writers' Conference, Kresge Arts in Detroit, and the Aninstantia Foundation. Tommye lives in his hometown of Detroit, Michigan.

ANA BOŽIČEVIĆ is a poet, translator, teacher, and occasional singer. She grew up in Zadar, Croatia, before coming to the States. Her most recent book is *New Life*. She is also the author of *Povratak lišća /Return of the Leaves*, Selected Poems in Croatian; *Joy of Missing Out*; the Lambda Award-winning *Rise in the Fall*; and *Stars of the Night Commute*. She received the 40 Under 40: The Future of Feminism award from Feminist Press, and the PEN American Center/NYSCA grant for translating *It Was Easy to Set the Snow on Fire* by Zvonko Karanović. She co-edited with Željko Mitić *The Day Lady Gaga Died: An Anthology of Newer New York Poets*.

OLGA BROUMAS is the author of several books of poetry, including *Rave: Poems, 1975–1999*. Her groundbreaking debut collection, *Beginning with O*, won the Yale Younger Poets Award. She has translated three books by Greek poet Odysseas Elytis.

JERICHO BROWN is author of the *The Tradition*, for which he won the Pulitzer Prize. He is the recipient of fellowships from the Guggenheim Foundation, the Radcliffe Institute for Advanced Study at Harvard, and the National Endowment for the Arts, and he is the winner of the Whiting Award. Brown's first book, *Please*, won the American Book Award. His second book, *The New Testament*, won the Anisfield-Wolf Book Award. He is the director of the Creative Writing Program and a professor at Emory University.

GABRIELLE CALVOCORESSI is the author of *The Last Time I Saw Amelia Earhart*, *Apocalyptic Swing* (a finalist for the *L.A. Times* Book Prize), and *Rocket Fantastic*, winner of the Audre Lorde Award for Lesbian Poetry. Calvocoressi is the recipient of numerous awards and fellowships including a Stegner Fellowship and Jones Lectureship, a Beatrice Shepherd Blane Fellowship at the Harvard-Radcliffe Institute, a Rona Jaffe Woman Writer's Award, a Lannan Foundation residency, the Bernard F. Conners Prize, and a residency from the Civitella di Ranieri Foundation. Calvocoressi is an Editor at Large at *Los Angeles Review of Books* and Poetry Editor at *Southern Cultures*. Calvocoressi teaches at the University of North Carolina–Chapel Hill and lives in Old East Durham.

KAYLEB RAE CANDRILLI is the recipient of a Whiting Award, a PEW fellowship, and of a fellowship from the National Endowment of the Arts. They are the author of *Water I Won't Touch, All the Gay Saints,* and *What Runs Over.* They live in Philadelphia with their partner.

CYRUS CASSELLS is the 2021–2022 Poet Laureate of Texas. Among his honors: a Guggenheim Fellowship, a Lambda Literary Award, the William Carlos Williams Award, and two National Endowment for the Arts grants. *Is There Room for Another Horse on Your Horse Ranch?* is his most recent book. He is a University Distinguished Professor of English at Texas State University.

DOROTHY CHAN is the author of five poetry collections, including *Return of the Chinese Femme.* They are an Associate Professor of English at the University of Wisconsin-Eau Claire and Co-Founder and Editor-in-Chief of Honey Literary Inc., a 501(c)(3) BIPOC literary arts organization run by women, femme, and queer editors of color.

JOS CHARLES is author of the poetry collections *a Year & other poems, feeld* (a Pulitzer Prize finalist and winner of the National Poetry Series), and *Safe Space.* She teaches for the University of California Riverside's Creative Writing Department and Randolph College's low-residency MFA program.

CHEN CHEN is the author of *Your Emergency Contact Has Experienced an Emergency* and a book of essays, *In Cahoots with the Rabbit God.* His debut book of poems, *When I Grow Up I Want to Be a List of Further Possibilities,* was longlisted for the National Book Award and won the Thom Gunn Award, among other honors. He teaches for the low-residency MFA programs at New England College and Stonecoast.

FRANNY CHOI is the author of *The World Keeps Ending, and the World Goes On; Soft Science;* and *Floating, Brilliant, Gone,* as well as a chapbook, *Death by Sex Machine.* She is a Lilly/Rosenberg Fellow, a recipient of Princeton's Holmes National Poetry Prize, and a graduate of the University of Michigan's Helen Zell Writers Program. The founder of Brew & Forge, a nonprofit whose mission is to foster relationships between writers and activists, Franny is a Poetry Editor at the *Massachusetts Review* and Faculty in Literature at Bennington College.

CODY-ROSE CLEVIDENCE is the author of *Listen My Friend This Is the Dream I Dreamed Last Night, Aux Arc / Trypt Ich, BEAST FEAST,* and *Flung/Throne,* as well as a few chapbooks. They live in the Arkansas Ozarks.

ANDREA COHEN is the author of eight collections of poetry, including, most recently, *The Sorrow Apartments.* She directs the Blacksmith House Poetry Series in Cambridge, Massachusetts.

HENRI COLE has published many collections of poetry and received numerous awards for his work, including the Jackson Poetry Prize, the Kingsley Tufts Award, the Rome Prize, the Berlin Prize, the Ambassador Book Award, the Lenore Marshall Award, and the Medal in Poetry from the American Academy of Arts and Letters. His most recent books are the memoir *Orphic Paris* and *Gravity and Center: Selected Sonnets, 1994–2022.* He teaches at Claremont McKenna College and lives in Boston.

CACONRAD has worked with the ancient technologies of poetry and ritual since 1975. They are the author of nine books, including *AMANDA PARADISE: Resurrect Extinct Vibration,* which won the 2022 PEN Josephine Miles Award. They received a 2022 Ruth Lilly Poetry Prize, a Creative Capital grant, a Pew Fellowship, and a Lambda Award. They exhibit poems as art objects with recent solo shows in Spain and Portugal, and their play *The Obituary Show* was made into a film in 2022 by Augusto Cascales. UK Penguin published two books in 2023, and a new collection of poetry is forthcoming from Wave Books in 2024 titled *Listen to the Golden Boomerang Return.*

EDUARDO C. CORRAL is the son of Mexican immigrants. His first book, *Slow Lightning,* won the Yale Series of Younger Poets competition. His most recent book is *Guillotine.* He's the recipient of residencies from the MacDowell Colony, Yaddo, and Civitella Ranieri. He's also the recipient of a Whiting Writers' Award, a National Endowment for the Arts Fellowship, the Hodder Fellowship and the National Holmes Poetry Prize. He teaches in the MFA program in Creative Writing at North Carolina State University.

BARBARA CULLY is the author of *The New Intimacy*, which won the National Poetry Series Award. She has published several additional poetry collections: *Desire Reclining, Shoreline Series, That Place Where, Back Apart, Under the Hours*, and *A Place Where One*. She is also co-editor of two writing textbooks, *Writing as Revision* and *Entry Points*. She taught for many years in the Department of English and Honors College at the University of Arizona, has been a guest writer at the Prague Summer Writing Program, and has been awarded the title Distinguished Adjunct Professor by Golden Gate University, San Francisco.

MEG DAY is the deaf, genderqueer author of *Last Psalm at Sea Level*, winner of the Publishing Triangle's Audre Lorde Award and a finalist for the Kate Tufts Discovery Award, and the co-editor of *Laura Hershey: On the Life & Work of an American Master*. The recipient of the Amy Lowell Poetry Traveling Scholarship and a National Endowment for the Arts Fellowship, Day teaches in the MFA Program at North Carolina State.

NATALIE DIAZ was born in the Fort Mojave Indian Village in Needles, California. She is Mojave and an enrolled member of the Gila River Indian community. She is the author of the poetry collections *Postcolonial Love Poem*, winner of the Pulitzer Prize, and *When My Brother Was an Aztec*. Her other honors and awards include the Nimrod/Hardman Pablo Neruda Prize for Poetry, the Louis Untermeyer Scholarship in Poetry, the Narrative Poetry Prize, and a Lannan Literary Fellowship.

ALEX DIMITROV is the author of three books of poetry, including *Love and Other Poems, Together and by Ourselves, Begging for It,* and the chapbook *American Boys*. He has taught writing at Princeton University, Columbia University, and New York University, among other institutions.

LISA DORDAL's most recent collections are *Water Lessons* and *Next Time You Come Home*. Her first book, *Mosaic of the Dark*, was a finalist for the Audre Lorde Award for Lesbian Poetry. She teaches at Vanderbilt University.

MARK DOTY is the author of nine books of poetry, including *Fire to Fire: New and Selected Poems*, which won the National Book Award; and *My Alexandria*, winner of the *Los Angeles Times* Book Prize, the National Book Critics Circle Award, and the T.S. Eliot Prize. He is also the author of four memoirs as well as a book about craft and criticism, *The Art of Description: World Into Word*. Doty has received two National Endowment for the Arts fellowships, as well as fellowships from the Guggenheim and Rockefeller Foundations, a Lila Wallace/Readers Digest Award, and the Witter Byner Prize.

JOSHUA JENNIFER ESPINOZA is a trans woman poet. She is the author of *I'm Alive / It Hurts / I Love It* and *THERE SHOULD BE FLOWERS*. Her third collection, *I Don't Want to Be Understood,* is forthcoming in 2024. She holds an MFA in poetry from UC Riverside and currently teaches creative writing. Jennifer lives in California with her wife, poet/essayist Eileen Elizabeth, and their dog and cat.

BLAS FALCONER is the author of, most recently, *Forgive the Body This Failure*. His awards include a National Endowment for the Arts Fellowship, the Maureen Egen Writers Exchange Award, a Tennessee Individual Artist Grant, the New Delta Review Eyster Prize for Poetry, and the Barthelme Fellowship. He is co-editor of *The Other Latin@: Writing Against a Singular Identity* and *Mentor & Muse: Essays from Poets to Poets*. He teaches in the MFA program at San Diego State University.

NIKKY FINNEY is the author of several books, including *Head Off & Split*, which won the National Book Award. Her most recent collection of poems is *Love Child's Hotbed of Occasional Poetry*. Finney is Carolina Distinguished Professor at University of South Carolina where she is also Director of the Ernest A. Finney Jr. Cultural Arts Center.

T'AI FREEDOM FORD is a New York City high school English teacher. t'ai has received awards and fellowships from Cave Canem, the Camargo Foundation, The Center for Fiction, Community of Literary Magazines and Presses, Kimbilio, The Poetry Project, and the Jerome Foundation. She is the author of two poetry collections, *how to get over* and *& more black*, finalist for the 2021 Kingsley Tufts Poetry Award, finalist for the Hurston-Wright Legacy Award, and winner of the Lambda Literary Award for Lesbian Poetry. t'ai lives and loves in Brooklyn where she is an editor at *No, Dear Magazine*.

BENJAMIN GARCIA is the son of Mexican immigrants, one of whom is formerly undocumented and one whose family has lived in New Mexico long before it was claimed by the United States. His debut collection, *Thrown in the Throat*, was a National Poetry Series selection.

SUZANNE GARDINIER is the author of twelve books, most recently *Amérika: The Post-Election Malas, Notes from Havana, Atlas*, and *The Spookmalas: Plan B(e)*. She teaches at Sarah Lawrence College.

ANDREA GIBSON is the author of five collections of poetry, including *Lord of the Butterflies*, which sold over 20,000 copies worldwide. The winner of the first Women's World Poetry Slam, Gibson has gone on to be featured on BBC, Air America, CSpan, and regularly sells out large capacity venues all over the world. Gibson has also released seven albums of spoken word. Their most recent book is *You Better Be Lightning*. They are the Poet Laureate of Colorado.

CARMEN GIMÉNEZ is the author of numerous poetry collections, including *Milk and Filth*, a finalist for the National Book Critics Circle Award, and *Be Recorder*, a finalist for the National Book Award, the PEN Open Book Award, the Audre Lorde Award for Lesbian Poetry, and the *Los Angeles Times* Book Prize. She has been awarded the Academy of American Poets Fellowship Prize, a Guggenheim Foundation fellowship, and has served as the publisher of Noemi Press for twenty years. She is Publisher and Executive Director of Graywolf Press.

NIKKI GIOVANNI is the author of numerous collections of poetry, essays, and books for children. She has received seven NAACP Image Awards and has been a finalist for the National Book Award. She is a University Distinguished Professor at Virginia Tech.

RIGOBERTO GONZÁLEZ is the author of eighteen books of poetry and prose. His awards include the PEN/Voelcker Award, the American Book Award from the Before Columbus Foundation, the Lenore Marshall Prize from the Academy of American Poets, and the Shelley Memorial Prize from the Poetry Society of America, and fellowships from the National Endowment for the Arts, the Lannan Foundation, the Guggenheim Foundation, and others. A critic-at-large for *The L.A. Times* and contributing editor for *Poets & Writers Magazine*, he is the series editor for the Camino del Sol Latinx Literary Series at the University of Arizona Press. Currently, he's Distinguished Professor of English and the director of the MFA Program in Creative Writing at Rutgers-Newark, the State University of New Jersey.

JAN-HENRY GRAY is the author of *Documents*, selected by D.A. Powell as the winner of the A. Poulin, Jr. Poetry Prize, and the chapbook *Selected Emails*. He's received fellowships from Kundiman, Undocupoets, and the Cooke Foundation. He was born in the Philippines and has lived in San Francisco, Seattle, Chicago, and Brooklyn. He is an Assistant Professor at Adelphi University in New York.

TORRIN A. GREATHOUSE is a transgender cripple-punk poet and essayist. She has received fellowships from the National Endowment for the Arts, the Effing Foundation for Sex Positivity, Zoeglossia, the University of Arizona Poetry Center, and the Ragdale Foundation. They are the author of *Wound from the Mouth of a Wound*, winner of the Kate Tufts Discovery Award, and *DEED*. She teaches at the Rainier Writing Workshop, the low-residency MFA program at Pacific Lutheran University.

MARILYN HACKER's eighteen books include *Calligraphies* and two collaborative books, *A Different Distance*, written with Karthika Naïr, and *DiaspoRenga*, with Deema K. Shehabi. She is translator of eighteen collections of French and Francophone poets. She received a Lambda Literary Award in 1994 for *Winter Numbers* and the Audre Lorde Award in 2001 for *Squares and Courtyards*.

JACK HALBERSTAM is Professor of Gender Studies and English and Director of the Institute for Research on Women, Gender and Sexuality at Columbia University. Halberstam is the author of seven books, including *Female Masculinity; In A Queer Time and Place; Gaga Feminism: Sex, Gender, and the End of Normal;* and *Wild Things: The Disorder of Desire.*

JAMES ALLEN HALL is the author of two books of poems, *Now You're the Enemy* and *Romantic Comedy*, selected by Diane Seuss for the Levis Prize. They have received awards from the National Endowment of the Arts, the Lambda Literary Foundation, the Texas Institute of Letters, and the Fellowship of Southern Writers. They are also the author of a book of lyric essays, *I Liked You Better Before I Knew You So Well*, which won the Cleveland State University Poetry Center Essay Collection Award. With Aaron Smith, they are the co-host of Breaking Form: A Podcast of Poetry and Culture. They teach at Washington College, where they direct the Rose O'Neill Literary House.

FRANCINE J. HARRIS' third collection, *Here is the Sweet Hand*, was a finalist for the Kingsley Tufts Award and winner of the 2020 National Book Critics Circle Award. She is Professor of English at the University of Houston and serves as Consulting Faculty Editor at *Gulf Coast*.

MARCELO HERNANDEZ CASTILLO's most recent book, *Children of the Land: a Memoir*, was a finalist for the International Latino Book Award. He is also the author of *Cenzontle*, winner of the A. Poulin Jr. prize, the Great Lakes Colleges Association's New Writer Award, and the Golden Poppy Award. He is a founding member the Undocupoets campaign which successfully eliminated all citizenship requirements from every major first book poetry prize in the nation. He was the first undocumented student to graduate from the Helen Zell Writers Program at the University of Michigan.

RICHIE HOFMANN is the author of two collections of poems, *Second Empire* and *A Hundred Lovers*.

SAEED JONES is the author of the memoir *How We Fight for Our Lives*, winner of the Kirkus Prize for Nonfiction, and the poetry collection *Prelude to Bruise*, winner for the PEN/Joyce Osterweil Award. His most recent book is *Alive at the End of the World*.

JOHN KEENE is a writer, translator, professor, and artist whose book *Punks: New & Selected Poems* received the National Book Award. He is also the author of *Annotations, Counternarratives*, and *Seismosis*, with artist Christopher Stackhouse, and a translation of Brazilian author Hilda Hilst's novel *Letters from a Seducer*. Keene is the recipient of many awards and fellowships, including the Windham-Campbell Prize, the Whiting Foundation Prize, the Republic of Consciousness Prize, the American Book Award, and a MacArthur Fellowship. He teaches at Rutgers University–Newark.

DONIKA KELLY is the author of *The Renunciations*, winner of the Anisfield-Wolf Book Award, and *Bestiary*, the winner of the Cave Canem Poetry Prize, a Hurston/Wright Legacy Award, and the Kate Tufts Discovery Award. Kelly has also received a Lannan Residency Fellowship and a fellowship from the Fine Arts Work Center. She is an assistant professor at the University of Iowa.

ROBIN COSTE LEWIS won the National Book Award for *Voyage of the Sable Venus*, her first collection of poetry. She is also the author of *To the Realization of Perfect Helplessness* and coauthor, with Kevin Young, of *Robert Rauschenberg: Thirty-Four Illustrations for Dante's Inferno*. The former poet laureate of Los Angeles, Lewis is currently writer in residence at the University of Southern California.

TIMOTHY LIU was born in San Jose, California, to immigrant parents from China. He is the author of numerous books, including *Down Low and Lowdown: Timothy Liu's Bedside Bottom Feeder Blues; Of Thee I Sing*, selected by *Publishers Weekly* as a Book-of-the-Year; *Say Goodnight*, which received a PEN Open Book Margins Award; and *Vox Angelica*, which won the Poetry Society of America's Norma Farber First Book Award. He has also edited *Word of Mouth: An Anthology of Gay American Poetry*.

RANDALL MANN is the author of six poetry collections, most recently *Deal: New and Selected Poems*. He is the recipient of the Kenyon Review Prize in Poetry and the J. Howard and Barbara M.J. Wood Prize from *Poetry*, and is a three-time finalist for the Lambda Literary Award. Mann lives in San Francisco.

JANET MCADAMS' new and selected poems, *Buffalo in Six Directions / Búfalo en seis direcciones*, was recently published in bilingual editions in Mexico and Argentina. Her other poetry collections include *Feral*, the chapbook *Seven Boxes for the Country After*, and *The Island of Lost Luggage*, which won both the Diane Decorah First Book Award from the Native Writers Circle of the Americas and an American Book Award. She is the founding editor of Salt Publishing's Earthworks Series of Indigenous Poetry and an emerita professor of Kenyon College, where she held the Robert P. Hubbard Chair in Poetry.

RACHEL MCKIBBENS is a Chicana poet, activist, playwright, essayist, and two-time New York Foundation for the Arts poetry fellow. She is the author of three books of poetry: *Pink Elephant, Into the Dark & Emptying Field,* and *blud.* McKibbens founded the Pink Door Writing Retreat, an annual writing retreat exclusively for women of color.

RACHEL MENNIES is the author of the poetry collections *The Naomi Letters* and *The Glad Hand of God Points Backwards*, winner of the Walt McDonald First-Book Prize in Poetry at Texas Tech University Press and finalist for a 2015 National Jewish Book Award. She is the series editor, since 2016, of the Walt McDonald First-Book Prize in Poetry and serves as assistant poetry editor and reviews editor for *AGNI*. With Ruth Awad, she edited the anthology *The Familiar Wild: On Dogs and Poetry.*

JANE MILLER'S most recent poetry books are *Who Is Trixie the Trasher? and Other Questions* and *Paper Banners*. Her essays, *From the Valley of Bronze Camels: A Primer, Some Lectures, & a Boondoggle on Poetry*, are in the Poets on Poetry Series, The University of Michigan Press. She is married to the artist Valyntina Grenier. They live in Tucson, Arizona.

DEBORAH A. MIRANDA is an enrolled member of the Ohlone-Costanoan Esselen Nation in California; she has Santa Ynez Chumash, English, and French lineage. In addition to *Bad Indians: A Tribal Memoir*, winner of the PEN Oakland Josephine Miles Literary Award, she is the author of four poetry collections, *Indian Cartography, The Zen of La Llorona, Raised by Humans,* and *Altar for Broken Things*, and she is co-editor of the Lambda finalist *Sovereign Erotics: An Anthology of Two-Spirit Literature.*

JONAH MIXON-WEBSTER is a poet, educator, scholar, and art activist from Flint, Michigan. He is the founder of the nonprofit Center for Imaginative Freedoms and Economic Relief (C.I.F.E.R.) and serves as chapter leader of PEN America-Detroit. His debut poetry collection, *Stereo(TYPE)*, received the PEN America/Joyce Osterweil Award and was a finalist for the Lambda Literary Award for Gay Poetry. He is the inaugural Mellon Arts Postdoctoral Fellow in African American and African Diaspora Studies at Columbia University, the recipient of the Windham Campbell Prize for Poetry and fellowships from Vermont Studio Center, Center for African American Poetry and Poetics, Images & Voices of Hope, The Conversation Literary Festival, and the PEN Writing for Justice Program.

RAJIV MOHABIR is the author of three collections of poetry, including *Cutlish*, which was awarded the Eric Hoffer Medal Provacateur, longlisted for the PEN/Voelcker Prize, and was a finalist for the National Book Critics Books Award. He also authored the memoir *Antiman*, which was a finalist for the PEN/America Open Book Award, Randy Shilts Award for Gay Nonfiction, Lambda Literary Award for Gay Memoir/Biography, and received the Forward Indies for LGBTQ+ Nonfiction. As a translator, his version of *I Even Regret Night: Holi Songs of Demerara* won the Harold Morton Landon Translation Award from the Academy of American Poets. He teaches in the creative writing program at the University of Colorado Boulder.

CARIDAD MORO-GRONLIER is the author of *Tortillera*, winner of the Texas Review Press Southern Poetry Breakthrough Series, and the chapbook *Visionware*. She is a contributing editor for *Grabbed: Poets and Writers Respond to Sexual Assault* and Associate Editor for *SWWIM Every Day*, an online daily poetry journal for women identifying poets. She resides in Miami, Florida, with her family.

MIGUEL MURPHY is the author of *Shoreditch* and two previous books of poetry. He lives in Southern California where he teaches at Santa Monica College.

Eileen Myles is a poet, novelist, and art journalist. Their most recent poetry collections are *I Must Be Living Twice: New and Selected Poems 1975–2014* and *Working Life*. They edited the anthology *Pathetic Literature*. Among their many honors are grants from the National Endowemnt for the Arts, a Guggenheim Fellowship, and the Shelley Award from the Poetry Society of America. They live in New York and Marfa, Texas.

Christopher Nelson is the author of *Blood Aria* and four chapbooks, including *Blue House*, recipient of a New American Poets Fellowship from the Poetry Society of America. He is the recipient of the 2023–24 Amy Lowell Traveling Scholarship and the founding editor of *Under a Warm Green Linden* and Green Linden Press, a nonprofit publisher dedicated to poetic excellence and reforestation. His anthology *Essential Voices: Poetry of Iran and Its Diaspora* received a Midwest Book Award and was named one of the best poetry books of the year by *Entropy Magazine*.

Jennifer (JP) Perrine is the author of four books of poetry: *Again; The Body Is No Machine; In the Human Zoo;* and *No Confession, No Mass*. A 2022 Oregon Humanities Community Storytelling Fellow and a 2022–23 Independent Publishing Resource Center Artist-in-Residence, Perrine lives in Portland, Oregon, where they cohost the Incite: Queer Writers Read series, teach writing, and guide nature-based mindfulness experiences.

Carl Phillips is the author of sixteen books of poetry, most recently *Then the War: And Selected Poems 2007–2020*, which won the 2023 Pulitzer Prize. Phillips has also written three prose books, most recently *My Trade Is Mystery: Seven Meditations from a Life in Writing*. He teaches at Washington University in St. Louis.

Tommy Pico is a poet, podcaster, and TV writer. He is author of the books *IRL, Nature Poem, Junk,* and *Feed*. Originally from the Viejas Indian reservation of the Kumeyaay nation, he now splits his time between Los Angeles and Brooklyn. He co-curates the reading series Poets with Attitude, co-hosts the podcast Food 4 Thot and Scream, Queen!, is poetry editor at *Catapult Magazine*, writes on the TV shows *Reservation Dogs* and *Resident Alien*, and is a contributing editor at *Literary Hub*.

Catherine Pond is the author of *Fieldglass*, winner of the Crab Orchard First Book Prize and a finalist for the National Poetry Series. With Julia Anna Morrison, she is the co-founder and co-editor of *Two Peach*.

D.A. Powell's books include *Repast, Useless Landscape or A Guide for Boys,* and *Chronic*. Powell received the 2019 John Updike Award from the American Academy of Arts and Letters. He teaches at the University of San Francisco.

Ruben Quesada is the editor of a hybrid collection, *Latinx Poetics: Essays on the Art of Poetry*. He is the author of *Jane: La Segua, Revelations,* and *Next Extinct Mammal: Poems*. He has received fellowships and grants from Canto Mundo, Lambda Literary Foundation, Virginia Center for the Creative Arts, Vermont Studio Center, and the Department of Cultural Affairs and Special Events at the City of Chicago. He is an Associate Fellow at the Attic Institute of Arts and Letters. He teaches in the MFA Program in Creative Writing at Antioch University–Los Angeles and for the UCLA Extension Writers' Program.

Justin Phillip Reed is the author of two poetry collections, *The Malevolent Volume* and *Indecency*, winner of the National Book Award. His most recent book, a hybrid collection, is *With Bloom Upon Them And Also With Blood: A Horror Miscellany*.

Boyer Rickel is the author, most recently, of *Morgan (a Lyric)*, winner of the Gold Line Press nonfiction chapbook contest. In addition to two poetry collections, *remanence* and *arreboles*, and a memoir-in-essays, *Taboo*, he has published three poetry chapbooks. His honors include poetry fellowships from The National Endowment for Arts and The Arizona Commission on the Arts, as well as awards for lyric essays from *Prairie Schooner* and *Tupelo Quarterly*. He taught in the University of Arizona Creative Writing Program for twenty years, serving as assistant director from 1991–2004.

Lee Ann Roripaugh is a biracial Nisei and the author of five volumes of poetry, mostly recently *tsunami vs. the fukushima 50*, which was named a "Best Book of 2019" by the New York Public Library, selected as a poetry Finalist in the Lambda Literary Awards, cited as a Society of Midland Authors Honoree in Poetry, and was named one of the "50 Must-Read Poetry Collections in 2019" by *Book Riot*. She was named winner of the Association of Asian American Studies Book Award in Poetry/Prose for 2004, and a 1998 winner of the National Poetry Series. The South Dakota State Poet Laureate from 2015–2019, Roripaugh is a Professor of English at the University of South Dakota, where she serves as Editor-in-Chief of *South Dakota Review*.

Kay Ryan's several books include *Elephant Rocks*; *The Best of It*, which was awarded the Pulitzer Prize; *Say Uncle*; and *Synthesizing Gravity: Selected Prose*. She served two terms as Poet Laureate to the Library of Congress and was a MacArthur Foundation Fellow. Her other major grants and prizes include the Ruth Lilly Poetry Prize and the National Humanities Medal, along with three Pushcart Prizes and awards from the Guggenheim Foundation and the National Endowment for the Arts.

Natasha Sajé is the author of five books of poetry, including *The Future Will Call You Something Else*; a postmodern poetry handbook, *Windows and Doors: A Poet Reads Literary Theory*; and a memoir, *Terroir: Love, Out of Place*. She teaches in the Vermont College of Fine Arts MFA in Writing Program and lives in Washington, DC.

Sam Sax is the author of *Madness*, winner of The National Poetry Series; *Bury It*, winner of the James Laughlin Award from the Academy of American Poets; and, most recently, *Pig*. They are the two-time Bay Area Grand Slam Champion. They have received fellowships from The National Endowment for the Arts, The Poetry Foundation, Yaddo, Lambda Literary, the MacDowell Foundation, and is a lecturer at Stanford University.

Maureen Seaton authored two dozen poetry collections, both solo and collaborative—recently, *Undersea* and *Sweet World*, winner of the Florida Book Award for poetry. Her honors include Lambda Literary Awards for both Lesbian Poetry and Lesbian Memoir, the Publishing Triangle's Audre Lorde Award, a fellowship from the National Endowment for the Arts, and a Pushcart Prize.

Rebecca Seiferle has published four poetry collections, including *Wild Tongue*, which won the Grub Street National Poetry Prize, and *Bitters*, which won the Western States Book Award. She has also published two translations from the Spanish of César Vallejo: *Trilce* and *The Black Heralds*. She has been awarded a Lannan Literary Fellowship and was Tucson Poet Laureate from 2012–2016.

Charif Shanahan is the author of two collections of poetry, *Trace Evidence: poems* and *Into Each Room We Enter Without Knowing*, a finalist for the Lambda Literary Award for Gay Poetry and the Publishing Triangle's Thom Gunn Award. He is an Assistant Professor of English and Creative Writing at Northwestern University.

Brenda Shaughnessy is the author of six poetry collections, including *Tanya*; *So Much Synth*; *Human Dark with Sugar*; and *Our Andromeda*, which was a finalist for the Kingsley Tufts Award, the International Griffin Prize, and the PEN Open Book Award. A Guggenheim Foundation Fellow, she is Professor of English and Creative Writing at Rutgers University–Newark.

Richard Siken is a poet, painter, and filmmaker. His book *Crush* won the 2004 Yale Series of Younger Poets prize, selected by Louise Glück, a Lambda Literary Award, a Thom Gunn Award, and was a finalist for the National Book Critics Circle Award. His other books are *War of the Foxes* and *I Do Know Some Things*, forthcoming in 2024. Siken is a recipient of a Pushcart Prize, two Lannan Fellowships, two Arizona Commission on the Arts grants, and a fellowship from the National Endowment for the Arts. He lives in Tucson, Arizona.

Jake Skeets is the author of *Eyes Bottle Dark with a Mouthful of Flowers*, winner of the National Poetry Series, the Kate Tufts Discovery Award, the American Book Award, and Whiting Award. He is from the Navajo Nation and teaches at the University of Oklahoma.

AARON SMITH is the author of five books of poetry, including *Stop Lying* and *Blue on Blue Ground*, winner of the Agnes Lynch Starrett Prize. A three-time finalist for the Lambda Literary Award, he is the recipient of fellowships from the New York Foundation for the Arts and the Mass Cultural Council. He is associate professor of creative writing at Lesley University in Cambridge, Massachusetts, and the co-host of Breaking Form: a Poetry and Culture Podcast.

DANEZ SMITH is the author of three collections, including *Homie* and *Don't Call Us Dead*. They have won the Forward Prize for Best Collection, the Minnesota Book Award in Poetry, the Lambda Literary Award for Gay Poetry, the Kate Tufts Discovery Award, and have been a finalist for the NAACP Image Award in Poetry, the National Book Critic Circle Award, and the National Book Award. They are the recipient of fellowships from the Poetry Foundation, Princeton, United States Artists, the McKnight Foundation, the Montalvo Arts Center, Cave Canem, and the National Endowment for the Arts.

CHRISTOPHER SOTO's debut poetry collection is *Diaries of a Terrorist*, which *Boston Globe* named one of the best books of 2022. He edited *Nepantla: an Anthology for Queer Poets of Color*. He has been honored with Them's Now Award in Literature for representing the cutting edge of queer culture.

BRIAN TEARE, a 2020 Guggenheim Fellow, is the author of eight chapbooks and six critically acclaimed books, including *Doomstead Days*, winner of the Four Quartets Prize and a finalist for the National Book Critics Circle Award. His most recent publications are a pair of book-length ekphrastic projects exploring queer abstraction, chronic illness, and collage: the 2022 Nightboat reissue of *The Empty Form Goes All the Way to Heaven*, and the fall 2023 publication of his seventh book, *Poem Bitten by a Man*. His honors include Lambda Literary and Publishing Triangle Awards, and fellowships from the National Endowment for the Arts, the Pew Foundation, and the MacDowell Colony. After over a decade of teaching and writing in the San Francisco Bay Area, and eight years in Philadelphia, he's now an Associate Professor of Poetry at the University of Virginia. He lives in Charlottesville, where he makes books by hand for his micropress, Albion Books.

TC TOLBERT (he/him/hey grrrl) is a trans and genderqueer poet who never ceases to experience a simultaneous grief and deep love any time s/he pays attention to the world. S/he writes, works with wood, learns, teaches, and wanders. In 2019, TC was awarded an Academy of American Poets' Laureate Fellowship for his work with trans, non-binary, and queer folks. Publications include *Gephyromania* and five chapbooks. TC is also co-editor (along with Trace Peterson) of *Troubling the Line: Trans and Genderqueer Poetry and Poetics*. *The Quiet Practices* won the Chad Walsh Chapbook Prize at *Beloit Poetry Journal*. TC lives in Tucson, Arizona, where s/he is the current Poet Laureate.

PAUL TRAN is the author of the debut poetry collection, *All the Flowers Kneeling*. Winner of the Discovery/Boston Review Poetry Prize, as well as fellowships from the Poetry Foundation, Stanford University, and the National Endowment for the Arts, Paul is an Assistant Professor of English and Asian American Studies at the University of Wisconsin-Madison.

DAVID TRINIDAD's books include *Digging to Wonderland: Memory Pieces*, *Notes on a Past Life*, and *Peyton Place: A Haiku Soap Opera*. He currently lives in Chicago.

VANESSA ANGÉLICA VILLARREAL was born in the Rio Grande Valley to formerly undocumented Mexican immigrants. She is the author of *Beast Meridian*, winner of the John A. Robertson Award for Best First Book of Poetry from the Texas Institute of Letters, and recipient of a Whiting Award and fellowship from the National Endowment for the Arts.

OCEAN VUONG is the author of the poetry collection *Time is a Mother*, the novel *On Earth We're Briefly Gorgeous*, which has been translated into 37 languages, and the critically acclaimed poetry collection, *Night Sky with Exit Wounds*, winner of the T.S. Eliot Prize, the Whiting Award, the Thom Gunn Award, and the Forward Prize for Best First Collection. Among his honors are a MacArthur Genius Grant and fellowships from the Poetry Foundation, the Lannan Foundation, the Civitella Ranieri Foundation, The Elizabeth George Foundation, and The Academy of American Poets. Born in Saigon, Vietnam, and raised in Hartford, Connecticut, in a working-class family of nail salon and factory laborers, he is a professor at New York University.

MICHAEL WASSON is the author of *Swallowed Light* and *This American Ghost*. A Ruth Lilly and Dorothy Sargent Rosenberg Poetry Fellow and a Native Arts and Cultures Foundation National Artist Fellow in Literature, he is nimíipuu from the Nez Perce Reservation in Idaho.

PHILLIP B. WILLIAMS is the author of *Mutiny* and *Thief in the Interior*, winner of the Kate Tufts Discovery Award and a Lambda Literary Award. He is the recipient of a fellowship from the National Endowment for the Arts, a Whiting Award, and a Ruth Lilly Fellowship. He serves as a faculty member at Bennington College and Randolph College low-res MFA.

SHELLEY WONG is the author of *As She Appears*, longlisted for the National Book Award and winner of the Lambda Literary Award for Lesbian Poetry. She lives in San Francisco.

MARK WUNDERLICH is the author of four books of poems: *The Anchorage, Voluntary Servitude, The Earth Avails,* and *God of Nothingness*. The recipient of fellowships from the Guggenheim Foundation, the National Endowment for the Arts, the Fine Arts Work Center in Provincetown, the Civitella Ranieri Foundation and elsewhere, he is the Executive Director of the Bennington Writing Seminars in Vermont and lives in New York's Hudson Valley.

C. DALE YOUNG practices medicine full-time and teaches in the Warren Wilson College MFA Program for Writers. He is the author of a novel in stories, *The Affliction*, and five collections of poetry, mostly recently, *Prometeo*. He is a recipient of fellowships from the Bread Loaf Writers' Conference, the National Endowment for the Arts, the John Simon Guggenheim Memorial Foundation, and the Rockefeller Foundation. He is the recipient of the Hanes Award from the Fellowship of Southern Writers.

MAGDALENA ZURAWSKI's most recent publications include *The Tiniest Muzzle Sings Songs of Freedom* and the chapbooks *Don't Be Scared* and *Being Human is an Occult Practice*. *Companion Animal* won a Norma Faber First Book Award from the Poetry Society of America. She is also the author of *The Bruise*, a novel. During the 2022–23 academic year she was a Fulbright Scholar in Poland, where she conducted research for a new book project on post memory. Zurawski teaches in the Creative Writing Program at the University of Georgia.

Permissions

Thank you to the authors who hold the rights to their poems and have granted permission to include their work in this anthology, and thank you to the following publishers who have allowed reprinting of previously published poems.

KAVEH AKBAR, "A Boy Steps Into the Water" and "Some Boys Aren't Born They Babble" from *Calling a Wolf a Wolf*. Copyright © 2017 by Kaveh Akbar. Reprinted with the permission of The Permissions Company, LLC on behalf of Alice James Books, alicejamesbooks.org.

DERRICK AUSTIN, "Remembering God After Three Years of Depression" and "Exegesis as Self-Elegy" from *Tenderness*. Copyright © 2021 by Derrick Austin. Reprinted with the permission of The Permissions Company, LLC on behalf of BOA Editions, Ltd., boaeditions.org.

CAMERON AWKWARD-RICH, "Faggot Poetics" from *Sympathetic Little Monster*. Copyright © 2016 by Cameron Awkward-Rich. Reprinted with the permission of Ricochet Editions. "Cento Between the Ending and the End" from *Dispatch*. Copyright © 2019 by Cameron Awkward-Rich. Reprinted with the permission of Persea Books, New York. All rights reserved.

RICK BAROT, "Whitman, 1841" and "On Gardens" from *Chord*. Copyright © 2015 by Rick Barot. Reprinted with the permission of The Permissions Company, LLC on behalf of Sarabande Books, Inc., sarabandebooks.org

ELLEN BASS, "Mammogram Callback with Ultrasound" and "Ode to Fat" from *Indigo*. Copyright © 2020 by Ellen Bass. Reprinted with the permission of The Permissions Company, LLC on behalf of Copper Canyon Press, coppercanyonpress.org.

ROBIN BECKER, "Dyke" from *Tiger Heron*. Copyright © 2014 by Robin Becker. Reprinted with the permission of the University of Pittsburgh Press.

MARK BIBBINS, three excerpts from *13th Balloon*. Copyright © 2020 by Mark Bibbins. Reprinted with the permission of The Permissions Company, LLC on behalf of Copper Canyon Press, coppercanyonpress.org.

FRANK BIDART, "Half-light" and "Queer" from *Half-Light: Collected Poems, 1965–2016* by Frank Bidart. Copyright © 2017 by Frank Bidart. Reprinted by permission of Farrar, Straus and Giroux. All Rights Reserved.

RICHARD BLANCO "Love as if Love" and "Maybe" from *Looking for the Gulf Hotel*. Copyright © 2012 by Richard Blanco. Reprinted with the permission of the University of Pittsburgh Press.

ANA BOŽIČEVIĆ, "Carpe Damn" and "Busted Xmas Card" from *Joy of Missing Out*. Copyright © 2017 by Ana Božičević. Reprinted with the permission of Birds, LLC.

OLGA BROUMAS, "Tryst" and "She Loves" from *Rave: Poems 1975–1999*. Copyright © 1989 by Olga Broumas. Reprinted with the permission of The Permissions Company, LLC on behalf of Copper Canyon Press, coppercanyonpress.org.

JERICHO BROWN, "As a Human Being," "Duplex ["The opposite of rape is understanding"]," "Stand," and "Bullet Points" from *The Tradition*. Copyright © 2019 by Jericho Brown. Reprinted with the permission of The Permissions Company, LLC on behalf of Copper Canyon Press, coppercanyonpress.org

GABRIELLE CALVOCORESSI, "Who Holds the Stag's Head Gets to Speak" and "Shave" from *Rocket Fantastic*. Copyright © 2017 by Gabrielle Calvocoressi. Reprinted with the permission of Persea Books, New York. All rights reserved.

342